FEASTS ❧ OF ❧ EDEN

Gracious Country Cooking from the
RED APPLE INN

FEASTS OF EDEN

Gracious Country Cooking from the
RED APPLE INN

Ruby C. Thomas

August House / Little Rock

P U B L I S H E R S

Published by August House, Inc.,
P.O. Box 3223, Little Rock, Arkansas, 72203,
501-372-5450

Printed in the United States of America

10 9 8 7 6 5 4 3 2 1

LIBRARY OF CONGRESS CATALOGING-IN-PUBLICATION DATA

Thomas, Ruby C., 1900-
Feasts of Eden: gracious country cooking
from the Red Apple Inn/
Ruby C. Thomas.—1st ed. p. cm.
ISBN 0-87483-111-3 (alk. paper): $24.95
1. Cookery. 2. Red Apple Inn. I. Title.
TX714.T494   1990
641.5—dc20   90-32654
CIP

First Edition, 1990

Cover Photograph by Thomas S. Gordon
Book Design and Production by Designed Communications
Typography by Lettergraphics
Project direction by Martin Thoma

Except for those otherwise credited, all interior
photographs are the work of Thomas S. Gordon.

This book is printed on archival-quality paper which meets the
guidelines for performance and durability of the Committee on
Production Guidelines for Book Longevity of the Council on
Library Resources.

AUGUST HOUSE, INC. PUBLISHERS LITTLE ROCK

Contents

Acknowledgments   9
Foreword   11
Introduction   13
A Note on Light Cooking   16

Images of Eden   *17*

Themes and Menus   *33*

Memorable Mornings: Breakfasts and Brunches at the Inn   35
Luncheons the Year Round   44
     Spring   45
     Summer   49
     Fall   52
     Winter   58
Afternoon Tea by the Fire   62
Poolside Parties and Casual Fare   66
"Dress for Dinner" at the Inn   79
Festive Occasions in the Gate Room   95
Holidays on the Island   122
     Easter   122
     Thanksgiving   125
     Christmas   130
     Independence Day   134

Other Favorite Recipes   *139*

Appetizers   141
Breads   144
Eggs, Cheese and Pasta Dishes   148
Soups   151
Salads   157
Meat   167
Chicken   175
Fish and Seafood   182
Vegetables   190
Soufflés   198
Sauces   202
Desserts   205

Index   212

*To Jack Gay, Elna Bolen, Pauline Jackson, Winsell Harris,
Anna Towle, Marian Watkins, Wanda Elslander, Nolan Bettis and
Margaret Wood and the many others who made fine dining
at the Red Apple Inn possible.*

*And to the thousands of guests of the Red Apple Inn whose
appreciation has made our work so rewarding.*

Acknowledgments

A profound thanks to all of the family members who worked on this cookbook: our daughter, Jean, who put it all together with the help of her husband, Walter Clancy; our grandaughters, Jane Gordon and Anne Gordon Atkinson, for their writing and editing work; our daughter Jane McGehee, our grandson Frank McGehee, Jr. and his wife Lisa McNeir; our son, Jim, and his wife, Lynn Thomas, and daughter, Mary Van Wyck, for food consultation, and thanks to all of them for sharing with me their memories of the Red Apple Inn.

Many others contributed to putting the book together: Geneva Jauck inspired me to undertake the book in the first place; Eloise Pearson gave us her collection of slides of Eden Isle that were so lovingly taken in the early years; Thomas S. Gordon provided the photographic illustrations; Natasha L. Grotenhuis did the food styling and layout design, David P. Conrad gave lighting and technical assistance; Anncha Briggs assisted with design; Phil Cato designed flower arrangements; Elizabeth Dowell kept us all in good humor. To all of these talented persons I owe a debt of gratitude.

RCT

Foreword

In the heart of Arkansas lies a treasure. For many this treasure remains unknown, buried in the wooded foothills of the Ozarks. For others this treasure has become a way of life, a welcome escape from a turbulent and fast–changing world.

Eden Isle, a resort bearing presumed resemblance to the garden of the same name, is a blend of sophistication and rustic beauty that has become, in the words of one travel writer, "the epitome of quiet luxury."

The entire island is landscaped to enhance the native wood and stone that graces it. Homes and buildings such as the Red Apple Inn, marina and condominiums reflect an architectural influence of southern Europe. Villas with tiled roofs are clustered against the hillsides. Other dwellings are made entirely from native stone, wood and glass. The rooms in the Inn are large and airy, with beamed ceilings and exquisite furnishings, mostly imported from Spain.

Waterfalls, landscaped terraces and stone and wrought–iron gates add an Old World charm to areas around the swimming pool, trails and eighteen–hole golf course. At Eden Isle one has the sense of being on the Spanish Riviera rather than in the middle of Arkansas. In fact, the island has been described as a "Mediterranean haven" in ads and travel brochures.

"Gracious country living" was the goal of Eden Isle's founders, a goal that has been met and sustained during the island's twenty-five-year history. Envisioned and brought into reality by Herbert L. Thomas, Sr., founder and chairman of the board of First Pyramid Life Insurance Company, and his wife, Ruby C. Thomas, Eden Isle began as a ragged expanse of undeveloped land near the quiet town of Heber Springs. The Thomases knew that the land had vast potential, particularly since the Corps of Engineers planned to build a dam, creating Greer's Ferry Lake, which would surround the land on three sides. Emphasizing quality, not profit, they created an "island" resort that became "unsurpassed in the Mid–South and equivalent to the finest available in the country," according to journalist Angus McEachran of the Memphis *Commercial Appeal.*

From its inception, Eden Isle was to be a place where food was celebrated. Take the apple, for instance. The apple has occupied a special place in history: as the Forbidden Fruit of the Garden of Eden and in American folktales of Johnny Appleseed. Recognizing the tempting beauty of the polished red MacIntosh apple, the Red Apple Inn began the custom of delivering a basket of these fresh apples to travelers arriving at the Inn. Besides providing nourishment, this welcoming gift set the tone of a holiday full of leisure, elegance and comfort. According to Assistant Manager Jack Gay, these are the finest eating apples anywhere, but are not always available in August when the supply of premium apples diminishes before the fall harvest. Several very special apple dishes are featured—the Red Apple Apple Pie, Apple Crisp and the Sweet Potato and Apple Casserole. Some customers say they come back year after year to the island because of those juicy red apples, a unique feature in the hotel business where even the most elegant would at best offer store–bought chocolates.

More customers return for the food served at the Red Apple Inn, whose well–known cuisine was originally an extension of the Thomas' own kitchen. In fact, one of the unique features of many of the sumptuous recipes used at the Inn is that they originated at home and were adapted for the restaurant. This process is, of course, a reversal. What we hope to offer with this cookbook is a way to bring the Red Apple cuisine into your home.

"Gracious country living" is perhaps *best* reflected in its cooking, and here we offer what we think is the best of our "paradise"—recipes that have brought distinction to Eden Isle that can now be enjoyed by your family and guests. We hope that when you discover this treasure, you will experience "Eden" too.

Jean Gordon and Walter Clancy
Anne Atkinson
Jane Gordon
Tom Gordon
Jane McGehee
Frank McGehee and Lisa McNeir

September, 1989

Introduction

My husband, Herbert Thomas, was a visionary. He always wanted to make things better in Arkansas by building something beautiful. When he heard about the creation of a new lake on the Little Red River at Heber Springs, he conceived of an island where people could spend leisure time in a natural setting graced with an elegant ambience. The first time he took me to the site and showed me the breathtaking views of the wooded valleys from the top of the crest, I exclaimed, "It's an Eden!"—and Eden Isle got its name.

The inspiration for the Red Apple Inn took root long before that, however, during a forty-two day Mediterranean cruise in 1954 with Henrietta and Sam Peck, owners and managers of the lovely old Sam Peck Hotel in Little Rock. They had furnished the hotel with antiques and interesting objects they had collected in their travels, and were always looking for ideas to make their hotel more personal and hospitable. Collecting antiques had always been a hobby of ours, and we were fascinated by their eye for the unusual in both furnishings and food.

Later, after we had decided to develop the island, Herbert and I toured the Costa Brava in Spain and fell in love with the beautiful coastline—its clusters of tile-roofed villas nestled on the sides of the mountains. It was then that the concept for Eden Isle jelled. The Spanish architecture of the houses overlooking the water complemented the natural beauty and created an atmosphere we wanted to replicate on the island.

We shopped in the antique shops in Barcelona's Old Town for furniture and furnishings and visited the Royal carpet factory outside of town, where we bought the rugs for the entire Inn. We even purchased fabrics for the draperies and bedspreads. When we finished, it took a whole ship to transport everything back to Arkansas.

We bought the rest of the furnishings in Mexico, where we found beautiful hand-carved reproductions of antique Mexican furniture. In a small suburb of Guadalajara, we found the terra cotta fireplaces that later warmed hands and toasted marshmallows on cool nights on the terrace of the Inn.

When all of these furnishings arrived on the island, they were placed in a large warehouse called "Ali Baba's Cave" by the construction workers. There was more than enough to furnish the Inn, and when the first islanders began completing their homes, they visited the cave to select decorative and architectural items.

Herbert Thomas had such strong views on the food he ate and how it should be served, you might have thought he spent most of his time at the dinner table. But he had strong views about everything, and was very active in the business and community life of Arkansas. He started the First Pyramid Life Insurance Company while in his twenties, and built several other businesses, including the City National Bank in Fort Smith and the Booneville Bank. Among his many activities were helping to acquire Little Rock's water supply system, managing Senator J. William Fulbright's first campaign for Congress, and serving as Chairman of the Board of Trustees of the University of Arkansas. He authored a billboard by the Main Street bridge that read, "Who Will Build Arkansas If Her Own People Do Not?" which gained national recognition during Little Rock's 1957 desegregation crisis when an *Arkansas Gazette* photographer captured it as the backdrop for the federal troops rolling into town. Building Arkansas was his passion. He was a man of vision and activism, and when he worked on a project, you knew something was going to happen. In later years, he remarked, "I always thought I could do it, even if I couldn't."

When he started talking about his dream for a resort on Greers Ferry Lake and before the lake had begun to fill, two of our children, Jane and Jim, flew over the property to see what he was talking about. Jane returned and reported that Dad had surely gone off the deep end this time. There was really nothing there but a cornfield surrounded by a lot of trees and rocks. And it was just that—the trees and rocks that had inspired his vision. He saw a mountain, sandstone cliffs and lichen–covered rocks. And he saw thousands of pine, flowering dogwoods, cedar, black gum and sweet gum trees.

Bob Shaheen, a young landscape architect from Little Rock, and David George, an architect and former student of Frank Lloyd Wright, helped Herbert draw up a plan for developing the island. The golf course and larger permanent homes would be built on the flat top of the island where the cornfield now was. The winding ledge of rock on the western side would become home sites high above the water. Clusters of villas would be built as weekend homes on the lower eastern side of the island around the marina. The Inn would also be high, overlooking the eastern side of the lake. David and Bob spent a whole day sitting and looking at the site for the Inn to decide its exact placement.

Herbert wanted to build the first cluster of Spanish–style villas by the lake to show prospective buyers. So he advertised a design contest for architects. Guy Ramsey, a young architect from Paragould, wanted the job. He bought several records of Spanish music and spent the weekend at a motel with his assistant listening to the music and drawing villas. He got the job, and Herbert built his villas. Five villas were built around a common driveway, facing away from each other for privacy. They were all of different size and material, some native stone and some stucco. All had fireplaces and used new and old wrought iron, glass and tile from Spain built into the patio walls or fountains, which gave them European charm. These villas set the tone for the houses that were subsequently built around the lake.

When the Inn was finished, we saw the need for a shop where people could buy the little necessities they had left at home, and also a place where they could browse for gifts and beautiful objects for furnishing their homes. I didn't know anything about running a business, but I did the buying for the shop and contracted for the First Pyramid to keep the books. Antiques, especially china, had always been a real love, and in my travels I bought for the shop. We also carried a few more trendy items, such as the huge china tiger I bought to add atmosphere to the store. I never thought it would sell, as it was very expensive. To my amazement, it sold immediately and we had to keep reordering. I learned that people wanted to buy something special when they were away from home and had the leisure time to shop.

The building and operation of Eden Isle was a famly affair, and all of our children became involved in some way. Our son, Herbert Jr. and son-in-law, Frank McGehee, were in business in the insurance company Herbert founded, and often had to help Herbert keep his eye on the bottom line.

Our other son, Jim Thomas, financed the building of the Inn, and spent a lot of time helping the island in many ways. Son-in-law, Frank Gordon, wrote poetry about the island and played music on Saturday night at the Inn. Our daughter, Jane, displayed her paintings of apples on the walls, and later taught art lessons to a dedicated group of women on the island. Our daughter, Jean, oversaw the dinner rolls. Jane and Jean later ran the gift shop together. Several of our twelve grandchildren had their first jobs waiting on tables in the dining room or working at the marina.

Many people from Chicago, New England and other colder areas have come to Eden Isle, looking for a milder climate in which to retire. They found Eden Isle to be quiet and rustic enough for relaxed living, but stimulating because of the interesting and diverse backgrounds of the people who have come here to live.

About three hundred families now live on the island, and have a very active community life. They enjoy many hobbies including fishing, golf, sailing, gardening, woodworking and painting. The fishermen and gardeners often trade fish for tomatoes and the golfers are always promoting a tournament.

Many of the island residents are avid golfers. The first nine holes were built on the original corn field along with the Inn during the early sixties. Later another nine holes were added. Architect Gary Panks blended the island's rolling hills, tree–lined corridors and majestic hilltop vistas into a course that is challenging to novice and expert alike.

In the early days of the island, Herbert and I lived at Northwinds, a pink stucco house with a red tile roof built on the highest point of the island. The house wrapped around the point and had magnificent views of the lake on three sides. The sunrises and sunsets were breathtaking. On the south side a waterfall fell from the topmost point to the swimming pool fifty feet below. During a storm the wind was so strong that the waterfall would spray backwards up into the air, inspiring the name "Northwinds."

The grandchildren loved to visit and had their own space including a kitchen on the lower floor, reached by an elevator from the main floor. We had a golf cart with a pink and white striped awning that the grandchildren (not yet of driving age) loved to drive around the island. Herbert Thomas put a sudden stop to that pleasure when Tom Gordon and Scott McGehee drove over a green on the golf course right after a rain. Anne Gordon Atkinson remembers the fun they had driving through ditches until someone toppled the three-wheeled cart. To the grandchildren, Eden Isle was an adventure.

We later built a smaller house, white stucco with a blue tile roof, on the western side of the island where we still had the view of the sunsets. Herbert loved flowers, and (some say) overplanted the yard in rhododendrons, azaleas, tulips, peonies, jonquils and tropicana roses. But we had an abundance of flowers to enjoy in the yard and bring in the house, or share with the neighbors who often brought us trout or homemade treats.

The marina has a long breakwater to protect the boats during heavy weather. Herbert had put handmade colored glass lanterns up and down the breakwater. He decided that it made a perfect walkway, and islanders could promenade up and down on Sunday afternoons as he had seen people do in Spain in the evenings. He hired the Heber Springs High School band to come play one Sunday afternoon. Everyone turned out for the event and enjoyed the chance to visit with their friends. Herbert sent word that people in Spain didn't stop to talk with their friends, but just smiled a greeting. He sometimes had a hard time making people conform to his ideas.

After Eden Isle was named, it seemed natural that we call the Inn "The Red Apple Inn". This is where we wanted to create tempting food in a quiet and beautifully natural setting. Food, and the enjoyment of leisurely meals together, had always been important in our relationship and in rearing our children. I have always enjoyed preparing a meal that satisfies all the senses. Now I had the opportunity to share with others the pleasures of relaxed dining.

We thought of bringing in well trained chefs from the surrounding cities. But we ended up working with talented local women who were eager to show that they could prepare the traditional southern dishes with the taste and elegance we were looking for. We added new dishes from our travels whenever we found something that would complement our southern cuisine. As we integrated these dishes into the menu, the cooks and I worked to perfect each dish and tested it before it was offered to our guests.

At the heart of the Red Apple Inn cuisine are fresh ingredients carefully prepared and superbly seasoned according to family recipes that have been tested and tried in our family over the years. For example, we had a custom of offering grits for breakfast every morning. One morning we served grits boiled in chicken stock (a favorite). The next morning we might alternate with highly seasoned fried grits. This is one example of an ordinary southern dish elevated by a simple extra touch.

Too often special family recipes get lost in the passage of time. I want to share with you the magic and excitement of our family recipes. I hope you enjoy them!

Ruby C. Thomas, 1989

A Note On Light Cooking:

The dishes in these recipes are presented as they are prepared at the Red Apple Inn. Most people like to enjoy their vacation at the Inn eating delicious food without worrying about the consequences. For everyday fare at home, you might be interested in lowering the calories a bit, without compromising the taste too much.

One way to reduce the calories is to use an old-fashioned Arkansas favorite—buttermilk. Buttermilk with fresh herbs can substitute for the mayonnaise in a cream salad dressing. Lowfat yogurt is a good substitute for cheese, sour cream, or whipping cream.

You might also try using lowfat milk instead of regular milk or cream. Part skim ricotta cheese is an excellent substitute for sour cream in any recipe. Wine or chicken broth can be substituted for butter in a dish calling for a sauté of onions or other vegetables.

Another substitute for a cream sauce is a slightly starchy vegetable such as carrots or turnips. Place in a blender and purée with a little chicken broth and herbs. A small bit of potato puréed in skim milk makes a creamy sauce or a soup.

Whether you use the recipes as written or make slight adjustments to accommodate your own diet, the results will undoubtedly be good!

On Using the Menus:

Some entries contained in menus in the Themes & Menus section may not be immediately followed by a corresponding recipe. In some cases, the entry is so self-explanatory that no recipe is required (such as Grapefruit and Orange Sections or Crisp Crackers) but is nonetheless suggested as an accompaniment to the menu.

In other cases, where a recipe is obviously required but is not found within the given menu, it is provided elsewhere in the cookbook and can be located using the index at the end of the book.

Images of Eden

Trout Amandine with Tropicana Rose

Spring Dinner (from left): Sweet Potato Croquettes; Spring Lamb with Baked Stuffed Onions; Hot Rolls; Mint Jelly

Red Apple Apple Pie

→Winter Lunch (clockwise from front):
Homemade Chili; Fresh Fruit Salad with
Poppy Seed Dressing; Corn Fritters

Fresh vegetables for soups and salads, with pasta and
Irish Soda Bread

*(front to back) Fried Chicken Southern Style; Black-Eyed Peas
with Green Tomato Pickle; Pone Bread; Rice Salad*

*←Afternoon Tea: English Toffee Cookies and
Jam Cake with Caramel Icing*

Cold Orange Soufflé with Chocolate Sauce

Breakfast (from left): Popovers; Potato Cakes; Codfish Balls; Salt Mackerel

→*Russian "Zakuska" Table (front to back):*
Kulebiaka; Buckwheat Blini with Sour Cream;
Molded Beet Salad; Charlotte Russe

Fall Lunch (clockwise from left): Zucchini with Tomatoes; Irish Soda Bread; Oysters Florentine; Three Cheese Soufflé

Chateaubriand with Steamed Vegetables

Chicken Salad Supreme

→ Christmas Dinner (clockwise from front): Roast Turkey with Cranberry Sauce; Eden Isle Corn Bread Dressing; Parsley Buttered New Potatoes; Scalloped Oysters; Brussels Sprouts in Consommé

Luncheon offerings: Relish Tray with Toasted Rolls and Angel Biscuits

Sunset over Greers Ferry Lake (photo by H.L. Thomas)

Themes
and
Menus

Memorable Mornings: Breakfasts and Brunches at the Inn

Morning meals are traditionally an important part of the southern lifestyle, with a variety of dishes and served on fine china. Our family has always shared this practice with friends and guests at the Inn.

In an era when seventy percent of Americans eat breakfast on-the-go, the Red Apple Inn offers a relaxed atmosphere where diners can enjoy the view of the lake while sampling homemade bread, fresh fruits and other treats that are hallmarks of Eden Isle breakfasts.

"Absolutely delicious!" is how Jane McGehee, my daughter, describes the home-made biscuits at the Inn. And longtime employees remember that Herbert would occasionally have to scold employees who devoured excessive numbers of them.

Grits are common breakfast fare in the South, and we like to "dress them up" by adding cheese or cooking them in chicken broth. We alternated with fried grits every other morning. Rather than the standard bacon-and-eggs fare, we suggest a fresh herbed omelet or pancakes with strawberry butter.

I remember once during the early days on Eden Isle when Herbert and I were preparing for a trip and we stopped by the Inn for breakfast. The sweet roll that we were served had obviously been purchased that day at a commercial bakery. He sent word to the kitchen that the bakery goods were to be made each day in our kitchen. When he returned a week later, he was served the commercial rolls again. So he asked me to supervise the kitchen at the Red Apple Inn. Breakfast was the beginning of my adventure with cooking at the Inn.

The menus selected here have a distinctly southern flavor that travelers to the Inn have enjoyed since its beginning. Some of them lend themselves to entertaining, while others are more casual and appropriate for family meals.

We think you'll find them all a little special. All are served with coffee or tea.

MENU

Fresh Herbed Omelet
Crisp Bacon
Popovers
Strawberry Preserves
Grapefruit and Orange Sections

Fresh Herbed Omelet
Serves 1

3 eggs
¼ teaspoon salt
¼ teaspoon black pepper
1 tablespoon butter
2 tablespoons Gruyére cheese, grated
2 teaspoons fresh chives, chopped
1 teaspoon fresh parsley, chopped
½ teaspoon fresh tarragon, chopped
1 fresh parsley sprig

Break the eggs into a small bowl. Add the salt and pepper, and beat 20 to 30 seconds with a fork, taking care not to overbeat.

Heat the omelet pan until it is very hot. Add the butter. As it is melting, it will begin to foam. When the foam subsides and it is almost to the point of coloring, pour the egg mixture into the pan. Stir the eggs with a fork.

When the eggs are set on the bottom but still moist on the top, sprinkle with the chives, parsley, tarragon and cheese. Tip the pan and roll the omelet with the fork onto a warm plate. Garnish with parsley.

Crisp Bacon

Sliced bacon

Cook bacon in the oven at 400° in a pan with a well around it that allows the grease to drain off. Cook until well browned (about 12 minutes) and drain well on paper towels.

Popovers

Makes 8 to 10

1 cup sifted flour
¼ teaspoon salt
2 eggs
1 cup milk
1 teaspoon melted butter

Sift flour and salt together. Beat eggs until foamy; add milk and melted butter. Mix with flour mixture and beat until it foams. Pour into a smoking hot, greased cast–iron muffin tin or popover pan, filling them ⅓ full, and bake at 400° 15 minutes. Turn down to 350° and bake another 15 minutes.

I think of *Popovers* as a New England dish (great with lobster and corn-on-the-cob!) They are also fun for breakfast. They should puff up nicely if you follow the instructions.

Strawberry Preserves

4 cups fresh strawberries, washed
   and capped
1½ cups water
6 cups sugar

Place berries in pan with water. Let come to full boil. Boil 5 minutes. Add sugar that has been warmed in pan in oven. Do not stir, but shake gently. Boil 15 minutes or until 3 drops fall from spoon. Pour into flat pan and let stand overnight.

MENU

Sunday Brunch Mock Omelet
Coffee Cake
Crisp Bacon
Melon Slices with Lime Juice
Tiny Broiled Sausages

Sunday Brunch Mock Omelet
Serves 8

8 to 10 slices bread (white, French, or whole wheat)
¾ pound cheddar cheese, grated
6 eggs
2 cups milk
1 teaspoon salt
Optional: dash nutmeg, dash cayenne
⅔ stick unsalted butter

Trim crusts and cube the bread. Butter a casserole dish and alternate layers of bread and grated cheese. Beat the eggs. Add milk, salt and optional spices. Pour mixture over bread and cheese. Refrigerate overnight. Next day, melt the butter and pour over top. Cover and bake at 300° 45 minutes. Uncover and bake about 15 minutes or until lightly browned.

Variation: Add cooked, crumbled sausage for a heartier dish and omit the broiled sausage.

For a crowd, the *Sunday Brunch Mock Omelet* is easy because it is made the night before and refrigerated.

Coffee Cake
Serves 8 to 10

1 tablespoon butter
½ cup sugar
1 egg
1 cup milk
2 cups flour
1 teaspoon baking powder
1½ teaspoons vanilla
1 teaspoon orange juice
½ cup brown sugar
1 cup raisins
1 cup pecans, chopped
Cinnamon

Cream sugar and butter together. Add egg, beat well. Add milk alternately with flour and baking powder. Add vanilla. Mix thoroughly. Spread on cookie sheet or shallow, square pan. Mix orange juice, brown sugar, raisins, pecans and cinnamon, and spread over top of dough. Bake 20 minutes at 350°. When brown, pour a little melted butter or margarine over the top of cake. Serve hot.

MENU

Grilled Ham and Red-Eye Gravy
Grits Cooked in Chicken Broth
Soft Scrambled Eggs
Angel Biscuits
Strawberry Butter
Fruits in Season

Grilled Ham and Red-Eye Gravy

Ham slices
Boiling water

Sauté ham in a skillet and keep it warm in the oven. Add boiling water to the skillet to make red-eye gravy.

Grits Cooked in Chicken Broth

Grits
Chicken broth
White pepper
Butter

Cook grits according to package directions, substituting chicken broth for water. If using canned broth, reduce salt by half. Season with white pepper and a pat of butter.

Soft Scrambled Eggs

Eggs
Butter
Cream
Salt and pepper

Beat eggs with a fork 20 to 30 seconds. Season to taste with salt and freshly ground pepper. Add a pat of butter to the skillet and warm. Pour eggs into the skillet and cook over gentle heat, stirring with a wooden spatula until they slowly thicken into a creamy custard. You may add a little cream at the end to stop the eggs from cooking.

Herbert was very particular about his scrambled eggs. They had to be very creamy and soft, and they were a side dish with most breakfasts.

Angel Biscuits
Makes about 18 biscuits

⅛ teaspoon dry yeast
2 tablespoons warm water
2 cups flour
⅛ teaspoon soda
½ teaspoon salt
1 heaping tablespoon baking
  powder
⅔ cups Crisco
1 cup buttermilk

Sprinkle yeast on warm water and let stand. Mix flour, soda, salt and baking powder well. Work in shortening until well mixed. Add buttermilk and mix. Add yeast mixture. Stir until well mixed and then knead with hands until ready to roll thin. Cut into biscuits and bake at 400° about 12 minutes or until well browned.

Strawberry Butter

2 sticks unsalted butter
1 cup sifted confectioners sugar
1 cup fresh strawberries or 1
  package frozen strawberries

Soften butter and add confectioners sugar. Whip until fluffy. Add strawberries. Mold in any shape, put in refrigerator to set. Serve with hot biscuits, pancakes or waffles.

A dear friend and former employee, Athenel Ellslander, gave us this recipe. It's delicious with the *Angel Biscuits.*

MENU

Codfish Balls with Grape Jelly
Banana Bran Muffins
Fresh Pineapple and Strawberries
Crisp Bacon

Codfish Balls
Serves 4

1 7-ounce can codfish
1 cup mashed potatoes
1 egg, beaten
Pepper to taste
Flour

Mix cod, potatoes, egg and pepper. Roll into balls about half the size of golf balls. Roll in flour. Fry in deep vegetable shortening (385° to 390°) until golden brown. Drain on absorbent paper and serve hot with grape jelly.

Codfish Balls were one of Herbert Thomas' favorite breakfast dishes. We used to order the canned cod from New England when it was not available locally. Dried codfish may be substituted. It should be soaked overnight, drained and patted dry before chopping to add to this recipe.

Banana Bran Muffins
Makes 24 small muffins

1 cup sifted flour
½ tablespoon salt
½ teaspoon baking soda
¼ cup shortening
½ cup sugar
2 eggs, well beaten
2 cups bran
½ cup buttermilk
6 bananas, sliced and mashed
Optional: ½ cup walnuts, chopped

Sift flour, salt and soda together. Cream the shortening and sugar. Add the eggs, bran and buttermilk. Add the bananas and walnuts and stir into mixture. Drop into greased muffin tins ¾ full and bake at 375° 30 minutes. Smaller muffin tins may be used. (Shorten cooking time accordingly.)

MENU

Salt Mackerel
Potato Cakes
Prune Sour Cream Coffee Cake
Crisp Bacon
Fruits or Berries in Season

Salt Mackerel
Serves 2 to 4

1 pound dried salt mackerel
Pepper to taste
½ cup butter
¼ cup lemon juice

Soak mackerel overnight in water. Drain and pat dry. Broil 8 minutes on each side, basting with melted butter. Season with pepper and serve with browned butter and lemon juice.

Another breakfast favorite of Herbert's was *Salt Mackerel.* I might add that breakfast was his favorite meal and he had lots of favorites!

Potato Cakes
Serves 4 to 5

2 cups mashed potatoes (may use leftovers)
2 green onions, chopped
1 egg
1 to 2 tablespoons flour (depending on consistency of potatoes)
Tablespoon or so vegetable oil for frying

Mix first 3 ingredients and add 1 tablespoon of flour to mixture, adding the extra tablespoon if mixture is too moist. Brush hands with flour and form patties or pones. Fry in hot vegetable shortening until brown—about 5 to 7 minutes.

Prune Sour Cream Coffee Cake
Serves 6 to 8

1½ cups dried prunes
1 teaspoon grated lemon rind
2 cups flour, sifted
1 teaspoon baking powder
1 teaspoon baking soda
½ teaspoon salt
1 cup butter, softened
1 cup sugar
2 eggs
1 cup sour cream
1 teaspoon vanilla
½ cup light brown sugar, firmly
   packed
½ teaspoon cinnamon
½ cup chopped walnuts

Pour boiling water over prunes. Let stand 15 minutes. Drain, pit and dice prunes. Add lemon rind, set aside. Grease and flour 9-inch tube pan. Sift together flour, baking powder, soda and salt. Remove ¼ cup and toss with prunes.

Cream butter and sugar until fluffy. Beat in eggs, one at a time. Slowly beat in flour mixture, alternately with sour cream and vanilla, beginning and ending with flour. Fold in prunes. Combine brown sugar, cinnamon and nuts. Turn ⅓ batter into pan. Sprinkle with ⅓ brown sugar mixture, repeat layering twice. Bake at 350° 55 minutes, or until done. Cool in pan on rack 10 minutes. Remove from pan.

Emajean Harvie serves this coffee cake and gets raves!

Luncheons the Year Round

"The view is spectacular—the food is superb," Ruth Malone Vaughan, author of several cookbooks, wrote of dining at the Red Apple in *The Ozark Cookbook*. And lunch is the time to enjoy the views changing with the seasons from the dining room— of the lake at a distance or a Spanish fountain in the courtyard right outside the window.

Lunch at the Red Apple Inn is a pleasant break in the day for area residents who may be entertaining a guest or just getting together for a visit. Guests at the Inn enjoy a light meal. Often special events are planned for the Tuesday bridge group or the men's golf luncheons, and the menus are tailored for the occasion.

Lunch seems to be more influenced by the changing seasons than any other, both from the standpoint of the food and by the changing ambience out-of-doors. Soups and salads start with what is in season. Light salads, cold soups and fresh vegetables speak of spring and warm summer days. Fall and winter mean a chill in the air and a warm fire to complement a more hearty soup or casserole. For this reason I have presented the luncheon menus by each of the four seasons. I hope you find them interesting.

In every season lunch at the Red Apple starts with the ice cold vegetable tray— scallions, radishes, celery, carrots and black olives. Next comes the bread tray. If and when any of our dinner rolls are left over, they are made into *Crispy Garlic Bread* by slicing them into quarter-inch slices and brushing with garlic flavored corn oil. They are then spread with a mixture made of 1/4 cup Parmesan cheese, 1/4 cup butter, 1 teaspoon Worcestershire sauce and a dash of garlic salt. We spread this on one side of each slice and toast them under a broiler until nicely browned and crisp. They are especially good with soups or salads. The same thing can be done with leftover French bread.

Spring on Eden Isle is especially breathtaking, with thousands of wild dogwoods scattered all through the woods and hillsides, wild cherry and the flowering crab apples that were planted in the early years. Travelers come to the island to enjoy the blossoms in March and early April.

On the lake the bass fishermen are out when the bass start to bite in early spring. They tell us the hybrid bass are as "sporting" to catch as any fish. When they school to look for shad, the water churns like the inside of a washing machine. Bringing one in is a real thrill, as they are reluctant to be caught!

In the dining room we emphasize fresh fruits and vegetables that are starting to become more plentiful in the markets.

MENU

Shrimp Mousse
Asparagus Vinaigrette
Lemon Muffins
Mango Sherbet

Shrimp Mousse
Serves 4 to 6

1 can frozen shrimp soup
1 envelope plain gelatin
½ cup cold water
½ cup celery, minced
½ cup cucumber, minced
¼ cup mayonnaise
3 tablespoons lemon juice
1 pound fresh or frozen shrimp (or crab or lobster)

Thaw soup. Soften gelatin in a small pan of cold water. Then set over heat on stove to dissolve. Combine soup, gelatin, celery, cucumber, mayonnaise, lemon juice and shrimp. Pour into mold and chill until firm. Unmold and serve, garnished with cucumber slices.

Asparagus Vinaigrette
Serves 4 to 6

1 pound asparagus
½ dill pickle, finely chopped
1 teaspoon capers, finely chopped
1 tablespoon sweet red pepper,
    finely chopped
1 teaspoon salt
¼ cup white wine vinegar
1 tablespoon scallion, finely
    chopped
1 tablespoon parsley, finely
    chopped
1 teaspoon hard-boiled egg white,
    chopped
¼ cup olive oil

Break off the white part of the asparagus stalks where they choose to snap. Place in the steamer basket and steam no more than 20 minutes. They should still be bright green, and flexible but not limp. Drain well and place on a towel.

Mix remaining ingredients together; marinate asparagus in dressing and chill. Serve 3 to 6 stalks on bed of lettuce. May be garnished with sliced raw mushrooms or hard-boiled egg slices.

Asparagus in the markets tells us spring has arrived—and we welcome its appearance!

Lemon Muffins
Makes 5 dozen miniature muffins

1 cup sugar
1 cup butter
4 egg yolks, well beaten
2 cups flour
2 teaspoons baking powder
1 teaspoon salt
½ cup lemon juice
4 egg whites, stiffly beaten
2 teaspoons grated lemon peel
Optional: ½ cup pecans, chopped

Preheat oven to 375°. Combine sugar and butter and cream until smooth. Add egg yolks and beat well. Sift dry ingredients together. Add dry ingredients alternately with lemon juice to creamed mixture, mixing well after each addition. Do not overmix. Fold in the egg whites and lemon peel. Fill greased miniature muffin tins ¾ full and bake about 18 to 20 minutes. Serve hot or cold.

Mango Sherbet
Serves 4

1 large ripe mango
2 cups water
Juice of 1 lime
½ cup honey or ¾ cup sugar

Blend in blender or food processor. Taste and add sugar if needed. Pour into freezer and freeze as directed. Any fresh fruits may be substituted, adding lemon juice to taste. If using fresh raspberries, press through a sieve after blending to remove the seeds.
Serve with 2 small *English Toffee Cookies*.

My granddaughter, Anne, makes fruit sherbets quickly in one of the new no–ice freezers.

MENU

Crab and Corn Bisque
Garden Salad with Oil and Vinegar Dressing
Corn Sticks
Paradise Pie

Crab and Corn Bisque
Serves 6

½ cup butter
½ cup green onion tops
1 teaspoon garlic
2 tablespoons flour
1¼ teaspoon creole seasoning
¼ teaspoon thyme
¼ teaspoon cayenne pepper
1 quart fish stock
4 ears fresh corn, cut from cob or 2
   12-ounce cans whole kernel corn
1½ cups whipping cream
1 pound crab meat

Melt butter in 3-quart saucepan over medium heat. Add onion and sauté until wilted. Stir in flour, seafood seasoning, garlic and thyme. Cook until flour begins to stick to pan. Blend in crab stock and corn and simmer gently 15 minutes. Slowly stir in cream and blend well. Carefully add crab meat. Remove from heat and let stand 30 minutes. Reheat gently in double boiler. Add dash of cayenne and ladle into bowls.

This is a deliciously rich soup. Milk or half-and-half can be substituted for the cream to reduce the calories.

Garden Salad

Serves 6

3 fresh tomatoes, peeled
1 large cucumber, peeled
½ purple onion, peeled
1 stalk celery, sliced
Dill weed
Boston lettuce

Peel tomatoes and quarter. Scrape cucumber with tines of a fork and slice thinly. Slice onion thin. Marinate in ½ cup *Oil and Vinegar Dressing* 1 hour before serving. Serve over bed of lettuce and sprinkle liberally with dill weed.

Oil and Vinegar Dressing

Makes 1 ⅓ cups

very good

⅔ cup olive oil
⅓ cup vegetable oil
⅓ cup vinegar
Juice of 1 lemon
1 teaspoon salt
¼ cup sugar
1 tablespoon paprika
Fresh black pepper, ground

Blend all ingredients until smooth.

Corn Sticks

Makes about 8 corn sticks

¼ cup flour
½ teaspoon salt
2 tablespoons sugar
1 cup cornmeal
2 teaspoons baking powder
⅛ teaspoon soda
1 cup buttermilk
2 well beaten eggs
1 tablespoon bacon fat

Preheat oven to 425°. Grease cast–iron corn stick pans and heat in oven. Mix first 6 dry ingredients. Gradually add buttermilk, eggs and bacon fat. Batter should not be too thick or too thin. Adjust with amount of sweet milk or flour. Fill corn stick pans ⅔ full, and bake about 10 to 12 minutes, until brown.

You may substitute the same amount of sweet milk for the buttermilk, but add to the batter 1 tablespoon of mayonnaise. The amount of sugar may be reduced also.

Paradise Pie
Serves 6

3 egg whites
1 cup sugar
20 soda crackers (small squares)
1 cup pecans, chopped
½ pint heavy cream, whipped
1 teaspoon vanilla
7 ounces grated coconut

Beat egg whites until almost stiff. Add sugar gradually, continuing to beat. Fold in crumbled crackers and nuts. Scrape into 9-inch pie pan that has been well buttered. Bake 20 minutes at 325°. Cool. Top with whipped cream flavored with vanilla, and sprinkle with grated coconut.

I first had this simple but delicious dessert 30 years ago in Booneville, Arkansas. It is still a favorite at the Red Apple. It is quickly made and freezes well.

Summertime is the busiest season on Eden Isle, of course, when families are enjoying the pleasures of water skiing and sailing, tennis, golf and swimming in one of the two beautiful pools. Party barges can be rented at the marina for all–day family outings or late afternoon parties. If none of these activities beckon, loafing is always an acceptable alternative!

Lunch is usually light and cool.

MENU

Cold Cucumber or Avocado Soup
Chicken Salad Supreme
Homemade Mayonnaise
Frozen Tomato Salad
Buttered and Toasted Rolls
Cold Orange Soufflé

Cold Cucumber or Avocado Soup
Serves 4

2 cucumbers or avocados, peeled
    and seeded
2 tablespoons lemon juice
1 clove garlic, chopped
1 cup chicken broth
1 cup heavy cream
Salt and white pepper to taste
3 tablespoons scallions or chives,
    chopped

Chop the cucumber or avocado in pieces, holding aside a small amount for garnish. Purée in food processor or blender. Taste for seasoning and chill. Garnish with scallions or chives.

Chicken Salad Supreme
Serves 8

2½ cups cold cooked chicken,
    diced
1 cup celery, chopped
½ cup scallions, thinly sliced
2 tablespoons parsley, minced
1 teaspoon salt
1 cup white grapes, sliced
1 cup mayonnaise
½ cup heavy cream, whipped
½ cup Durkee's dressing
½ cup toasted almonds, shredded

Combine and serve in lettuce cups with thin slices of chicken on top and garnish with stuffed or thinly sliced ripe olives.

This salad can be made in a gelatin ring mold as follows: Add 1½ tablespoons gelatin, 4 tablespoons water and ½ cup chicken stock. Mix the chicken, celery, grapes, almonds, parsley and salt. Soak gelatin in the cold water 5 minutes and dissolve in hot chicken stock. When cold, add mayonnaise and whipped cream. Stir until thick and fold in the chicken mixture. Pack in individual molds or a large ring. Serve garnished with your favorites—artichoke hearts, for example.

Homemade Mayonnaise

1 whole egg
1 egg yolk
Salt and cayenne pepper to taste
1 teaspoon dry mustard
1 tablespoon lemon juice
Optional: 1 tablespoon red wine
    vinegar
1 cup vegetable oil and olive oil

Put eggs, salt and pepper, mustard, lemon juice and ¼ cup oil in blender or food processor. Blend briefly and then add remaining oil in a steady stream until thick. Turn off blender immediately. 1 teaspoon grated onion may be substituted for mustard.

Frozen Tomato Salad
Serves 6

6 large tomatoes, peeled and chopped
4 tablespoons sweet red pepper, chopped
1 tablespoon onion, chopped
4 tablespoons green peppers, chopped
2 tablespoons gelatin
2 tablespoons cold water
3 tablespoons vinegar
1 tablespoon lemon juice
1 tablespoon horseradish
1 teaspoon sweet basil
Salt and cayenne pepper to taste

Place tomatoes, red pepper, onion and green pepper in bowl of food processor and blend long enough to chop coarsely. Soften gelatin in cold water and place over pan of hot water to dissolve. Add to ingredients in bowl. Season with vinegar, lemon juice, horseradish, salt and cayenne and blend well. Pour into refrigerator tray and place in freezer 3 hours. Serve on lettuce with mayonnaise.

Buttered and Toasted Rolls

Leftover dinner rolls
Garlic–flavored corn oil
¼ cup Parmesan cheese
¼ cup melted butter
1 teaspoon Worcestershire sauce
Dash garlic salt

Slice rolls into ¼-inch slices, brush each slice in garlic flavored corn oil. Mix Parmesan, butter, Worcestershire sauce and garlic salt, and spread on one side of each slice. Toast under a broiler until nicely brown. We serve these for lunch or with soups and salads. The same thing can be done with leftover French bread.

We first had this bread in a beautiful hotel in La Jolla, California. Herbert liked the recipe so well he paid the waiter $5 for the recipe.

Cold Orange Soufflé
Serves 8 to 10

4 eggs
3 egg yolks
6 tablespoons sugar
1 ½ tablespoons gelatin
2 teaspoons lemon juice
3 tablespoons water
2 large oranges
2 cups heavy cream, whipped
½ cup red currant jelly, strained

Place eggs, yolks and sugar in electric mixer or food processor and beat until thick. Soften gelatin in lemon juice and water in small pan. Heat until dissolved. Carefully stir gelatin mixture into egg mixture with grated rind and juice of 1 orange. Fold in whipped cream. Tie a band of waxed paper around an 8-inch soufflé dish. Pour in mixture and let set in refrigerator about 2 hours. Remove and arrange around the edge skinned sections of other orange. Dip a soft brush into jelly and carefully cover top of soufflé with a layer of jelly. Chill again and remove paper just before serving. Serve with a bowl of *Chocolate Sauce* to ladle over each serving.

Fall travel in the Ozarks is a wonderful experience—and of course a trip to the Ozarks would not be complete without a visit to Eden Isle. The island is covered with sugar maples that were planted in the early days for dramatic red and yellow displays up and down the roadways and in the woods. The Red Apple Inn is a perfect spot to enjoy the autumn foliage juxtaposed against the blue of the lake on a sunny, cool day.

Because the wind on the lake picks up in September, the sailboats are out in large numbers. The Red Apple Marina has become quite a mecca for sailors with over a hundred boats anchored in slips. Races are held every other week. The Commodore's Regatta is held on the last Saturday in September and a two–day race is held in the middle of October for October Fest. Participants come from several states.

When the days get a little cooler, I think of a little heavier, and perhaps more earthy, food. Here are a few luncheon menus we might serve in the fall.

MENU

Shrimp and Artichoke Heart Casserole
Green Bean Salad
Irish Soda Bread
Coconut Cake

Shrimp and Artichoke Heart Casserole
Serves 8

2 pounds large shrimp, boiled and peeled
1 can artichoke hearts, drained and sliced
2 tablespoons butter
3 tablespoons flour
1 cup light cream
1 cup milk
½ teaspoon paprika
1 tablespoon catsup
1 tablespoon lemon juice
1 tablespoon Worcestershire sauce
1 tablespoon sherry
Dash of tabasco
1 cup Monterey Jack cheese, grated

Put alternate layers of cooked shrimp and sliced artichoke hearts in a buttered casserole. In a saucepan melt the butter and stir in the flour. Stir in the milk and cream over low heat, and stir constantly until the sauce has thickened. Add all of the remaining ingredients except the cheese and mix until well blended.

Pour over shrimp and artichoke hearts. When ready to serve, add grated cheese and heat in the oven until the sauce is bubbling and the cheese has melted and browned lightly. Garnish with fresh parsley sprigs.

This dish may be prepared well ahead of time and baked just before serving.

Green Bean Salad
Serves 6

2 pounds fresh green beans
1 tablespoon salad oil or olive oil
2 small onions, sliced
1 tablespoon wine vinegar

String beans and steam about 12 minutes, until tender but still green. Separate sliced onions into rings and add to beans. Add remaining ingredients, salt and toss lightly. Cover and marinate in refrigerator 3 to 4 hours.

Just before serving, add 3 tablespoons chopped olives or chives and 3 tablespoons chopped parsley. Then add a dressing made of these ingredients: ⅓ cup sour cream, 1 tablespoon horseradish, ⅓ cup mayonnaise, (dash of garlic optional).

Irish Soda Bread

2 cups white bread flour
1 cup whole wheat flour
1 level teaspoon salt
1 level teaspoon soda
1 cup buttermilk

Sift dry ingredients together and mix with milk to make a soft dough. Knead swiftly and lightly and form into a round loaf and place on buttered baking pan. With a knife, mark the top with a cross. Bake at 450° 30 minutes on the center shelf of oven.

Herbert and I rented a cottage in Ireland several summers and different family members visited us there. One of the pleasures we had was the soda bread which accompanied every meal.

Coconut Cake

Serves 8 to 10

3 cups flour
3½ teaspoons baking powder
¼ pound butter
½ cup milk
½ cup water
1½ cup sugar
½ teaspoon vanilla
4 egg whites, stiffly beaten

Sift flour once, measure; add baking powder and sift together 3 times. Cut butter into small pieces and cut into flour with a pastry blender. Mix milk and water and add with sugar and vanilla. Beat until smooth. Fold in egg whites and bake in 2 greased and floured cake pans at 375° 25 or 30 minutes. Remove from oven and allow to cool thoroughly. Slice each layer across, making 4 layers.

COCONUT ICING:
2 cups sour cream
2 cups granulated sugar
2 packages frozen coconut

Mix quickly and spread each layer with icing and cover entire cake. Place in refrigerator until serving.

MENU

Oysters Florentine
Zucchini with Tomatoes
Hot Buttered French Bread
Lemon Angel Pie

Oysters Florentine
Serves 8

1 quart shelled oysters with liquor
6 tablespoons butter
¼ cup onion, chopped
2 cups chopped spinach, well drained
Salt and pepper to taste
⅛ teaspoon nutmeg
2 tablespoons parsley, chopped
3 tablespoons flour
¼ cup cream
½ teaspoon garlic salt
1 tablespoon lemon juice
½ cup bread crumbs, buttered
2 tablespoons fresh Parmesan cheese, grated

Melt 2 tablespoons butter in skillet and add onion and spinach. Season with salt and pepper, nutmeg and parsley, simmer a few minutes and set aside. In a saucepan melt 4 tablespoons butter and make a cream sauce with the flour, oyster liquor and cream, stirring until smooth and thick. Add lemon juice and garlic salt. Spread the spinach mixture on the bottom of a large flat greased casserole dish. Lay oysters on top of spinach in one layer and cover with cream sauce. Top with buttered bread crumbs and cheese. Bake in 400° oven 20 minutes until bubbly and golden.

Zucchini with Tomatoes
Serves 8

1 to 2 pounds zucchini
1 pound red, ripe tomatoes
1½ tablespoons olive oil
½ cup onion, finely chopped
1 teaspoon garlic, finely minced
1 tablespoon chopped fresh basil or ½ teaspoon dried basil
Salt and freshly ground pepper to taste

Trip off the ends of the zucchini and cut the vegetables into 1-inch thick rounds. If the zucchini are very small, leave the rounds intact. If they are medium–size, cut the rounds in half. Peel the tomatoes and cut them into 1-inch cubes. In a heavy skillet, heat the oil and add the onion. Cook, stirring, until onion is wilted and add the garlic, tomatoes, basil, salt and pepper to taste and cook about 5 minutes. Add the zucchini and cover. Cook about 15 minutes. The zucchini should be tender yet crisp.

Lemon Angel Pie
Serves 6

4 egg whites
¾ cup sugar
1 ¼ teaspoon cream of tartar

Beat whites until frothy. Add cream of tartar. Continue beating, gradually adding sugar until mixture is stiff. Spread in an ungreased 9-inch pie tin and bake at 300° 1 hour. Cool.

FILLING:
6 egg yolks
¾ cups sugar
½ teaspoon salt
3 tablespoons orange juice
3 tablespoons lemon juice
1 teaspoon grated orange rind
1 teaspoon grated lemon rind

Beat egg yolks and sugar together in top of double boiler. Add remaining ingredients.

Cook over hot water, stirring until thick. Cool and spread over baked meringue. Cover with whipped cream and toasted slivered almonds.

MENU

Crab Soufflé
Fresh Fruit Salad with Poppy Seed Dressing
Corn Fritters
Hot Buttered French Bread
Chocolate Angel Pie

Crab Soufflé
Serves 4

3 tablespoons butter
3 tablespoons flour
1 ½ cups milk
1 ⅓ cups grated cheddar cheese
1 pound lump crab meat (3 cups)
4 eggs, separated
Salt and cayenne pepper to taste

Melt butter in saucepan and stir in flour until blended. Add milk slowly, stirring with a wire whisk. Continue cooking until thick. Melt cheese in cream sauce. Add crab meat and egg yolks, lightly beaten. Stir. Remove from stove and season to taste. Fold in stiffly beaten egg whites. Put into a 1 ½ quart soufflé dish. Set in pan of warm water and bake at 350° about 40 minutes.

This main dish soufflé is on the luncheon menu, but must be ordered at least an hour ahead of time. It is a favorite for birthday luncheons.

Poppy Seed Dressing
Makes 1 ¾ cups

¾ cup sugar
1 teaspoon dry mustard
1 teaspoon salt
⅓ cup vinegar
1 ½ tablespoons onion juice
1 cup vegetable oil
1 ½ tablespoons poppy seeds

In a blender or electric mixer, combine sugar, mustard, salt and vinegar. Grate the cut side of a white onion to obtain the onion juice. Or the onion may be blended in a food processor and strained. (Prepare to weep in either case!) Blend thoroughly and add oil slowly, beating constantly, and continue to beat until thick. Add poppy seeds and beat a few minutes. Store in the warmest part of the refrigerator. If it gets too cold or too hot, it will separate.

Serve over fresh fruit salad. Any fruits in season are delicious—some cut into chunks, some sliced and some in balls with an assortment of colors, and served on fluffy lettuce.

This dressing is especially good on combinations which include grapefruit.

Corn Fritters
Makes about 12

6 ears fresh corn, grated
½ cup flour
¼ teaspoon salt
2 teaspoons baking powder
2 eggs
½ cup powdered sugar, sifted

Mix well and form into balls. Fry in deep fat (375°) until well browned. Roll in powdered sugar and serve hot.

Corn Fritters are a natural with fruit salad. A dear friend, Jewel Bird taught me how to make them.

Chocolate Angel Pie
Serves 6

2 egg whites
Pinch of salt
½ cup sugar

Beat 2 egg whites with pinch of salt until foamy. Gradually add ½ cup sugar, beating until it stands in peaks. Spread in Pyrex pie pan. Bake at 200° 2 hours. Cool.

FILLING:
1 6-ounce package chocolate chips
2 tablespoons water
½ pint heavy cream, whipped

Melt chips in top of double boiler. Add water and remove from fire. When almost cooled, beat chocolate into whipped cream. Pour into baked pie shell and let stand 3 hours in the refrigerator.

Winter is a quieter time at the Inn, but delightful. A few couples we know love to come and stay in a room with a fireplace and enjoy the woods and scenery outdoors and the coziness indoors. One morning after a heavy snow, Elna Bolen was the only employee who showed up at work. A tree had fallen over her car and she had walked to a neighbors to borrow a chain saw, cut the tree off the car, and arrived at work on time. Katy and Frank Lambright had come up from Little Rock the day before to enjoy the snow with their children (while everyone else was driving the other way hoping to reach home before the snow was too deep) and he ended up helping Elna make the biscuits in the kitchen.

The floor-to-ceiling windows in the dining room encourage bird watching up close to the feeders just outside and in the open sky. The island is a paradise for bird watchers, with numbers of species. Families of road runners have made their nests along the rock escarpments. Guests have often spotted bald eagles soaring in the distant sky out the large north window of the dining room. With the trees bare of leaves, the blue of the lake is much more visible from the Inn.

MENU

Homemade Chili
Crisp Crackers, Fritos
Sweet Pickles, Dill Pickles, Olives and Celery
Apple Cake with Hot Buttered Rum Sauce

Homemade Chili
Serves 12

2 large onions, chopped
2 cloves garlic, chopped
¼ cup vegetable oil
3 pounds ground beef
2 #2 cans tomatoes
2½ cups beef broth
1 bay leaf
1 tablespoon chili powder
1 teaspoon salt
¼ teaspoon ground cloves
1 can kidney beans
1 tablespoon cornmeal
1 cup cheddar cheese, grated

Sauté onions and garlic in oil. Add ground beef and stir well until brown and grains separate. Add tomatoes, beef broth and bay leaf. Let simmer slowly 2 hours. Add chili seasoning, salt, cloves and kidney beans. Taste for seasoning. Just before serving add cornmeal while stirring. Garnish with grated cheese.

When the weather turns cold we often serve chili for lunch on Saturday.

Apple Cake with Hot Buttered Rum Sauce

½ cup butter
2 cups sugar
2 eggs
2 cups all purpose flour, sifted
1 teaspoon baking powder
¾ teaspoon baking soda
1 teaspoon salt
1 teaspoon nutmeg
1 teaspoon cinnamon
3 apples, pared, cored and
　　chopped
1½ cup nuts, chopped

Cream butter, gradually add sugar and beat until light and fluffy. Beat in eggs, one at a time. Sift together flour, baking powder, soda, salt, nutmeg and cinnamon. Gradually add to egg mixture. Dough will be fairly stiff. Stir in apples and nuts. Turn into buttered 9×13-inch pan. Bake at 325° 55 to 70 minutes.

SAUCE:
1 cup sugar
½ cup butter
½ cup half-and-half
3 teaspoons rum
Whipped cream

Combine sugar, butter and cream. Warm over low heat, stirring occasionally, until hot. Stir in rum. Serve over cake and top with whipped cream.

MENU

Vegetable Soup
Cracker Balls
Skillet Corn Bread
Brownie Pie

Vegetable Soup
Serves 8 to 10

1 large soup bone
2 onions, chopped
1 cup celery, chopped
4 cups tomatoes
2 turnips, chopped
½ cup cabbage, chopped
½ cup carrots, coarsely sliced
½ cup okra, sliced
2 tablespoons oatmeal
Beef stock to taste
2 bay leaves
Salt and pepper to taste
1 teaspoon Beau Monde seasoning
1 teaspoon chili powder
1 tablespoon pickling spices, tied in
   a cloth bag

Put soup bone in a large kettle in 1 gallon cold water to simmer. When meat is nearly tender, add vegetables and seasonings. Skim off most of the fat. Simmer until vegetables are cooked, about 30 minutes.

Cracker Balls

2 tablespoons butter, softened
1 egg
1 tablespoon milk or soup
½ teaspoon salt
Nutmeg and pepper to taste
1 tablespoon chopped parsley
6 tablespoons cracker crumbs

Stir butter with egg, add liquid and seasoning and enough crumbs to shape into small balls. Let stand ½ hour to swell. Drop into boiling beef, chicken or vegetable soup 10 minutes before serving.

My sister, Mazie Fuess, used to add cracker balls to vegetable soup—delicious!

Skillet Corn Bread
Serves 4 to 6

1 ½ cups white cornmeal
3 tablespoons all–purpose flour
1 ½ tablespoons baking powder
1 teaspoon salt
½ teaspoon soda
1 ½ cups buttermilk
3 eggs, beaten
2 tablespoons shortening

Sift together cornmeal, flour, baking powder, salt and soda into bowl. Melt shortening in 10-inch ovenproof skillet or 9-inch square baking pan in preheated 450° oven. Add milk and egg to dry ingredients, stirring to combine. Add melted shortening to batter; mix. Pour batter into the hot skillet or pan in which shortening was melted. Bake 20 to 25 minutes.

Brownie Pie
Serves 8

2 sticks butter or margarine,
   softened
4 tablespoons cocoa
2 cups sugar
1 ½ cups flour
4 eggs, beaten slightly
1 cup pecans or walnuts
8 marshmallows

ICING:
4 tablespoons cocoa
1 box powdered sugar
1 stick butter or margarine
4 tablespoons light cream

Cream butter, cocoa and sugar. Add flour and mix well. Add eggs one at a time and mix well. Add nuts. Pour into greased and floured 13×9×2-inch pan. Bake at 350° until done, but not dry. Cover with marshmallows and return to oven to melt. Remove from oven and cool in pan. Ice.

Mix until creamy and spread on pie.

Afternoon Tea by the Fire

Although few Americans have adopted the custom of having "afternoon tea" enjoyed so much by the British, Eden Isle has encouraged and maintained the tradition by offering tea (free to guests) every afternoon. Teatime is especially popular in the winter in front of the fire.

A variety of teas (both black tea and herbal) are served, along with *English Toffee Cookies,* which have become enormously popular—at tea and on other occasions.

My daughter, Jean Gordon, who makes the cookies at Christmastime and for other social gatherings, says that she cannot make enough of them. "Even when I freeze them for later, they disappear as soon as someone discovers them," she says.

Granddaughters, Anne and Jane, agree that these cookies are one of the best reasons for coming home to Mom's.

English Toffee Cookies

½ cup butter
½ cup margarine
1 cup sugar
1 egg yolk
1 teaspoon vanilla
2 cups flour
½ teaspoon salt
1 egg white, beaten
2 cups chopped pecans

Blend butter and sugar in food processor or electric mixer until creamy. Add egg yolk and vanilla and blend. Add flour and salt and blend. Let dough stand in refrigerator at least 30 minutes. With the palm of your hand spread very thin on cookie sheet, covering it completely. Lightly brush with beaten egg whites. Sprinkle with chopped pecans. Bake at 375° 12 to 15 minutes or until light brown. Let cool about 5 minutes and cut into small rectangles.

Macadamia Nut Balls

¼ pound butter
¼ pound margarine
1 cup sugar
1 egg
1 teaspoon vanilla
1 cup ground macadamia nuts
1¼ cups flour
⅛ teaspoon salt
1 cup powdered sugar, sifted

Cream butter and sugar together. Add egg and beat. Add remaining ingredients mixing well. Let dough sit in refrigerator at least 20 minutes. Roll into balls the size of a walnut, place on a cookie sheet and bake in a 375° oven about 12 minutes or until slightly brown. Cool a few minutes and carefully roll each ball in powdered sugar.

These cookies are rich with the flavor of macadamia nuts, but are so light they really do melt in your mouth.

Tuiles Aux Amandes
(Lacy Curved Almond Wafers)
Makes about 45 3-inch wafers

Rapidly mixed and baked, the wafers crisp almost immediately into the shape of old-fashioned roof tiles when they are lifted from the baking sheet to a rolling pin or bottle to cool. The only tour de main involved here is that you work out your own system for removing the wafers as quickly as possible from baking sheet to rolling pin; as they cool, they become too crisp to mold. Bake one sheet at a time, even though you may prepare several sheets in advance, or be baking one while you are preparing another.

3½ tablespoons butter
½ cup sugar
¼ cup egg whites (about 2 egg whites)
5 tablespoons cake flour
⅓ cup ground, blanched almonds
¼ teaspoon almond extract
½ teaspoon vanilla
½ cup sliced, shaved or slivered almonds

Preheat oven to 425°, and set rack in middle level. Butter baking sheets.

Beat butter and sugar together until soft and fluffy; add the egg whites, and beat a few seconds, enough to blend. Sift the flour over the batter, folding it in with a rubber spatula. Fold in the ground almonds, almond extract and vanilla. Using rubber spatula to dislodge batter, drop ½ teaspoon gobs onto one of the buttered baking sheets, spacing them 3 inches apart. With back of spoon, smear out each blob into a circle 2½ inches in diameter. Batter will be so thin you can see baking sheet through it. Add to each circle a pinch of sliced, shaved or slivered almonds.

Baking and shaping: Place in middle level of preheated oven, and set timer for 4 minutes. Wafers are done when a ⅛-inch border around circumference has browned lightly. Set baking sheet on

open oven door so that cookies will keep warm and pliable. Working rapidly, slide long side of spatula blade under one cookie to scrape and lift it off the baking sheet, and place right side up on rolling pin or bottle. Quickly continue with the rest; the wafers crisp to shape so quickly that the first several may be removed to rack to make room for remaining wafers. (If last wafers have cooled too much for molding, return sheet to oven several seconds to soften them).

Close oven door and wait a few minutes for temperature to return to 425°. Bake and mold the rest of the wafers in the same manner.

(Wafers will stay crisp for several days in dry weather when stored airtight; otherwise, freeze them).

My family and I enjoyed these Almond Tuiles at a lovely old château on the Tarn River in Southern France several years ago. They were molded in the shape of small dishes and held raspberry sorbet. They go nicely with fruit desserts, ices and afternoon tea.

Sour Cream Chocolate Cake
Serves 8 to 10

4 ounces bitter chocolate
1 cup hot water
2 eggs
2 cups sugar
1 cup sour cream
2 cups bread flour, sifted
1 teaspoon baking soda
½ teaspoon salt
2 teaspoons vanilla

Melt chocolate with hot water over low heat. Cream eggs and sugar throughly. Add sour cream, and mix. Add flour, soda and salt. Combine chocolate mixture with egg mixture. Add vanilla. Pour into 2 greased and floured 8-inch cake pans. Place in cold oven. Set oven at 300°, and bake 30 to 35 minutes. (Or cake may be baked 50 to 60 minutes in 9×13-inch pan.) Cool and ice.

ICING:
2 cups sugar
¼ cup cocoa
1 tablespoon white Karo syrup
½ cup milk
½ cup butter or margarine
1 cup pecans, chopped
1 teaspoon vanilla

Mix sugar and cocoa in saucepan. Add margarine, Karo and milk. Bring to boil. Boil 2 minutes. Cool 5 minutes. Beat until thick enough to spread. Add pecans and vanilla. Spread between layers and on top of cake.

For special occasions we might serve a very rich cake—and this one is very rich!

Jam Cake
Serves 10

¾ cup butter
1 cup sugar
3 eggs, separated
½ cup buttermilk
1 teaspoon soda
1 teaspoon each salt, cinnamon,
   allspice
2 cups flour
1 cup strawberry jam
½ cup chopped pecans

Cream butter and sugar, and add egg yolks, beating after each one. Add buttermilk. Sift soda, spices and flour together and add to mixture, mixing well. Fold in jam and pecans. Fold in stiffly beaten egg whites. Bake at 350° 30 to 40 minutes, or until top springs back when tapped. Allow to cool. Ice with *Caramel Icing*.

CARAMEL ICING:
½ cup sugar
2½ cups sugar
2 eggs
2 tablespoons butter
¾ cup milk
½ teaspoon salt

Brown ½ cup sugar in heavy iron skillet. Mix 2½ cups sugar, 2 whole eggs, and beat well. Add butter, milk, salt. Add the browned sugar. Cook slowly until it forms soft ball in cold water, stirring all the time. Take from fire and beat until ready to spread on cake.

My niece, Margaret Hastings, gave me this delicious *Jam Cake* recipe.

Buttermilk Pound Cake

½ pound butter
2 cups sugar
6 eggs, separated
1½ teaspoon vanilla
3 cups flour
1 cup buttermilk
½ teaspoon soda
1 cup sugar

Preheat oven to 325°. Grease and flour a 10-inch bundt pan. Cream butter and 2 cups sugar. Add beaten egg yolks and vanilla. Add flour alternately with buttermilk to which soda has been added. Mix well. Beat egg whites until stiff, slowly adding 1 cup sugar. Fold into cake batter. Bake in bundt pan 1 hour and 15 minutes. Cool on wire rack.

For a much less sinful sweet for tea, *Buttermilk Pound Cake* is good. Our neighbor and good friend, Cecil Robertson, loved this cake buttered and toasted for breakfast.

Poolside Parties and Casual Fare

Just below the Inn a rustic stairway leads down the hill, past a waterfall to the swimming pool, seeming to be just as nature made it. In reality, nature was enhanced a little bit by a young artist and landscape architect, Bob Shaheen, who worked with Herbert in the early days to create the "Eden Isle look." Bob knew how to enhance the natural look of the rolling hills and rolling rock formations on the island with split rail fences, wildflowers, native rock and wood chips in landscaping. In fact, it was Bob who discovered David George, the Dallas architect and student of Frank Lloyd Wright, who designed the Red Apple Inn and set its tone of rustic, contemporary charm and elegance.

Bob vividly remembers a party by the pool that he and his partner, Curt Goodfellow, staged a New England clam bake for the country club members and island residents. They ordered lobsters and clams from Maine and built a big fire to boil the lobsters and make a big pot of clam chowder by the pool just below where the Inn was being built. The party was a huge success—except for the clams, which were new to most of the local residents. After the party Bob and Curt and his family cleaned up and went home to bed. Bob said he suddenly awakened about 3:30 a.m. to see a giant blaze of fire out his window. His first thought was they hadn't put out the fire and the Inn was burning down. He and Curt were panicked. But when they arrived on the scene, devasting as it was to see the country club burning to the ground, at least they knew they hadn't been the cause. I remember Bob comforting me as we watched the devastation.

The building was about half destroyed, and we lost many of the antiques we had brought from Europe—one beautiful ruby red glass chandelier I especially remember.

The next morning Bob, my son, Jim and Herbert were standing looking at the smoldering fire and at the Inn which had been almost finished. They knew we had to have a place to serve food to the visitors to the Inn, and came up with the idea of a tent, perhaps on the parking lot. Bob insisted that the tent be by the pool below the

waterfall—and it turned out to be a great idea. In ten days' time an eye-catching green-and-white-striped tent signalled the return of meal service; it became a symbol for the relaxed conviviality islanders and visitors have enjoyed there over the years.

Lunches and informal dinners were served in the tent and outdoors by the pool. Children had a special dinner menu for "Seedlings up to age nine." The recreation room for teens was called the "Worm Hole." Islanders used the pool area for parties—several weddings even took place there—and many picnics and barbecues.

We started serving the Reuben sandwich that is still served at the Inn. And Dr. Jim Shelton's basting sauce became even more famous.

Here are a few of the casual meals we have enjoyed in the tent or by the pool.

MENU

Reuben Sandwich
Hot Mustard Sauce
Crudités
Pineapple Milk Sherbet

Reuben Sandwich
Serves 1

2 slices dark rye bread
2 slices cooked corned beef
½ cup sauerkraut

Spread *Hot Mustard Sauce* on one side of each slice of rye bread. Add corned beef and sauerkraut. Grill and serve hot with cold slivers of celery, carrots and scallions.

Hot Mustard Sauce

1 cup sugar
1 cup vinegar
1 cup dry mustard
2 eggs, well beaten

Mix sugar, vinegar and mustard in top of double boiler over hot water. Add beaten eggs and stir well. Simmer 1 hour until thick.

Pineapple Milk Sherbet
Serves 10

1 cup unsweetened pineapple juice
1 teaspoon grated lemon rind
¼ cup lemon juice
1 cup sugar
⅛ teaspoon salt
4 cups chilled milk

Combine and stir first 5 ingredients. Slowly stir these into the milk and freeze according to directions on your freezer.

Make up the mixture the day before you freeze it, to increase the yield and produce a smoother, creamier mixture.

This is a light dessert for lunch.

Occasionally we would have what we call a real "Southern country" meal. On the farm this used to be standard fare at lunchtime, but changing lifestyles have made this strictly a supper meal today. Any vegetable dishes can be substituted, such as succotash—and we'll include the recipe for that.

MENU

Fried Chicken Southern Style
Turnip, Mustard and/or Kale Greens
Black-Eyed Peas with Green Tomato Pickle
Wilted Lettuce
Pone Bread
Corn on the Cob
Apple Crisp

Fried Chicken Southern Style
Serves 3 to 4

2 ½ pound fryer
1 quart buttermilk
Salt and black pepper
2 cups flour
1 teaspoon paprika
3 cups vegetable shortening

Two hours before serving cut chicken into 8 pieces—2 drumsticks, 2 thighs, 2 breasts and 2 wings. Soak in buttermilk at least 1 hour. Remove and shake off excess milk. Mix salt, pepper, flour and paprika in paper bag or bowl. Add chicken pieces, a few at a time and coat thoroughly with flour mixture. Heat shortening to 375° in Dutch oven or heavy iron skillet. Add as many pieces of chicken as will fit comfortably without crowding. Brown 2 minutes on each side. Turn heat down, cover skillet and cook 10 minutes. Remove lid, turn heat to high and cook a couple of minutes until crisp. Remove and drain well on paper towels. Place in a low oven to keep warm.

Turnip, Mustard and/or Kale Greens
Serves 4 to 6

2 ½ pounds assorted tender greens
1 quart water
¼ pound salt pork
Pepper vinegar

Thoroughly wash greens and remove tough stalks. Boil briskly 10 to 45 minutes, depending on whether you like the Southern version, well-done with lots of "pot likke" or if you prefer them lightly cooked. If they are fresh-from-the-garden tender, they are delicious lightly cooked. Season with pepper vinegar.

Black-Eyed Peas
Serves 4 to 6

2 pounds unshelled black-eyed
   peas, or 2 packages frozen
1 onion, chopped
½ pound ham hock
1 teaspoon sugar
Salt and pepper to taste
Optional: dash of jalapeño pepper

Shell and wash peas, if fresh, and boil all ingredients in water to cover until tender. Purple hull or lady peas are delicious, too.

Black-eyed peas are standard fare in the south with turnip greens. They are a must on New Year's Day when they guarantee good luck for the coming year.

Green Tomato Pickle

1 peck green tomatoes, thinly sliced
½ cup salt
3 quarts cider vinegar
1 quart water
12 cups sugar
3 tablespoons pickling spice, tied in cloth
3 bay leaves
4 green bell peppers, seeded and sliced
6 cups onions, peeled and thinly sliced

Cover tomatoes with salt and let stand overnight. Combine the vinegar, water, sugar, pickling spice and bay leaves and bring to a boil. Add peppers, onions and drained green tomatoes. Bring to a boil and cook about 1 hour until liquid is reduced to half, stirring occasionally. Seal in sterilized jars or freeze in airtight containers. A small batch will keep in the refrigerator indefinitely.

Green Tomato Pickle is a relish I learned to make from my Southern mother-in-law. We enjoyed it all winter long with black-eyed or purple hull peas. Herbert did not often come into the kitchen to cook, but I remember him, with his sleeves rolled up, slicing tomatoes for this dish that he loved.

Wilted Lettuce
Serves 6

2 bunches fresh garden lettuce
6 slices crisp bacon, chopped
Salt and freshly ground black pepper to taste
¼ cup vinegar
1 teaspoon sugar
½ cup bacon drippings
6 scallions, chopped
4 eggs, hard-boiled and chopped

Wash and dry lettuce and chill in refrigerator. Fry bacon until crisp, drain on paper towel. Add vinegar, sugar and salt and pepper to bacon grease in skillet. Tear lettuce into large pieces in salad bowl. Sprinkle with bacon, scallions and eggs. Pour hot dressing over all and toss lightly. Serve immediately.

Wilted Lettuce is a dish that signals the arrival of spring. It is almost a meal in itself.

Pone Bread

Serves 4 to 6

Boiling water
2 cups cornmeal
½ teaspoon salt
Optional: 1 teaspoon butter, pinch
  of sugar, vegetable oil

Pour sufficient amount of boiling water (approximately 3 cups) over meal to scald every grain of meal. Add salt, sugar and butter. Stir vigorously until thoroughly mixed. When cool enough to handle, pat into pones ½ inch thick and fry in hot oil until brown. Turn and brown other side.

Alternate method: Pat into pones and bake in a hot oven. If using this method, preheat a baking pan to which you have added 1 tablespoon of oil. Bake at 400° until brown on the bottom and crisp on top.

Apple Crisp

Serves 8

3 pounds tart cooking apples
2 tablespoons butter
2 tablespoons lemon juice
Grated rind of 1 lemon
1 cup brown sugar
½ cup butter
½ teaspoon salt
½ teaspoon cinnamon
1 cup flour

Peel, core and slice apples into a buttered 14×14-inch pan. The apple layer when cooked should be about ¾ inch thick. Dot apples with butter and sprinkle with lemon juice and rind. With pastry knife work together sugar, butter, salt, cinnamon and flour. Sprinkle this mixture evenly over the apples. Bake about 30 to 40 minutes at 375°. Serve hot with vanilla ice cream or whipped cream on top.

When the islanders all gathered for an outdoor barbecue, Dr. Jim Shelton was the head chef. He marinated meats in his sauce recipe for at least a day ahead of time. He says it's great on all kinds of meat, and the islanders must have agreed. To this day they haven't elected a new chef!

MENU

Grilled Chicken with Dr. Shelton's Famous Basting Sauce
Deviled Rib Bones
Rice Salad
Garden Collage
Carrot Cake

Grilled Chicken

Serves 12

6 2- to 3-pound fryers, split in half

Wash and dry chickens and let soak overnight in Dr. Shelton's marinade. Remove chicken and broil on a hot grill over coals. Turn and baste with marinade every 15 minutes. Cook until tender, about 45 minutes.

Dr. Shelton's Famous Basting Sauce

1 quart white vinegar
1 ⅓ cup water
2 heaping teaspoons cayenne pepper
2 teaspoons paprika
2 teaspoons salt
2 teaspoons sugar

Heat to combine—do not boil. Keep warm for basting. This is delicious on any kind of meat!

Deviled Rib Bones

Serves 2 to 4

4 freshly roasted beef rib bones
Salt and pepper to taste
2 tablespoons English or Dijon
    mustard
3 tablespoons cream
1 cup fine bread crumbs
3 tablespoons melted butter

Sprinkle bones with salt and pepper. Make a thin paste with the mustard and cream and coat the bones. Sprinkle with bread crumbs, covering completely. Dot with butter and place under broiler until crisp and crusty, turning to brown all sides.

"Serve hot," says the chef, "and come to terms with fingers!"

Rice Salad

Serves 10 to 12

1 6-ounce package chicken flavored
    rice
1 16-ounce can artichoke hearts,
    drained and sliced
½ cup vinaigrette dressing
4 green onions, sliced with tops
8 stuffed olives
½ green pepper, chopped
⅓ cup mayonnaise
½ teaspoon curry powder

Cook rice according to directions, omitting butter. Cool. Marinate artichokes in vinaigrette dressing at least 2 hours. Add other solid ingredients and toss well with rice mixture. Serve well chilled.

To serve as a molded ring, rub the inside of an 8-inch ring mold lightly with mayonnaise and spoon mixture into mold. Chill until firm. Loosen around side of mold with a knife and turn onto a round platter. Center of mold may be filled with cherry tomatoes and fresh basil.

This is a good dish to serve to a large crowd. Other vegetables, such as lightly cooked beets or carrots, may be added.

Garden Collage
Serves 8 to 10

2 tablespoons butter
1 tablespoon olive oil
1 clove garlic, pressed
1 medium onion, chopped
1 bell pepper, chopped
1¼ pounds yellow squash (or 2 cups, thinly sliced)
2 cups fresh corn, cut from cob
10 new potatoes, scrubbed and partly peeled
2 tomatoes, peeled and diced
1 teaspoon salt
Pepper to taste
Pinch of sugar
½ cup chicken broth
1 tablespoon pesto

In a very large skillet, melt butter and sauté the garlic, onion and pepper until soft. Add squash and cook briefly before stirring in corn, tomatoes and seasonings. Put mixture into a buttered 2½– to 3-quart casserole and add water or chicken broth. Bake covered about 40 minutes at 350° or simmer on top of the stove. Casserole may be uncovered during the last 15 minutes to reduce the "pot likker." In place of the pesto any herbs may be used for seasoning such as basil, marjoram and thyme. This dish can be prepared ahead of time and reheated.

Carrot Cake
Serves 8 to 10

2 cups sugar
1½ cups vegetable oil
4 eggs
2 teaspoons cinnamon
2 teaspoons soda
1 teaspoon salt
2 cups bread flour, sifted
3 cups carrots, finely grated
1 cup English walnuts or pecans, chopped

Mix sugar and oil. Add eggs one at a time, beating after each addition. Add cinnamon, soda and salt. Mix well and add flour. Combine carrots and nuts and add to batter. Pour into two 9-inch greased and floured cake pans which have been lined with brown paper. Bake 40 to 45 minutes at 350°. Cool completely before frosting.

FROSTING:
¼ pound butter, softened
1 8-ounce package cream cheese, softened
1 box powdered sugar, sifted
1 tablespoon lemon juice
1 tablespoon vanilla
1 cup nuts, chopped

Combine butter, cream cheese, sugar, lemon juice and vanilla and blend in a food processor or mix with beater until smooth. Add nuts and mix well. Frost cake and keep cool in refrigerator.

MENU

Fried Catfish
Tartar Sauce
Hush Puppies
Cabbage Slaw
La Fonda Pudding

Fried Catfish
Serves 6

**6 9- to 11-ounce catfish, cleaned
and dried**
Salt and pepper to taste
2 cups cornmeal
Vegetable oil

Add salt and pepper to cornmeal. Coat catfish well with mixture. Fry at 375° until well browned and drain on paper towels.

Catfish used to be a southern fish. In the last few years it has become popular all over the country. It provides high protein with very little fat, and is very flavorful. Chefs are inventing new ways of cooking the filets that are available now, and they are delicious. This is the traditional southern fried catfish recipe—perhaps unsophisticated, but very tasty.

Tartar Sauce

1 cup mayonnaise
**2 tablespoons sweet pickle,
chopped**
**2 tablespoons green olives,
chopped**
2 tablespoons onion, chopped
1 tablespoon capers, chopped
2 tablespoons parsley, chopped

Mix well and serve with fried fish.

Hush Puppies
Makes about 12

2 cups cornmeal
¾ teaspoon salt
¼ cup green onions, finely chopped
    (green part and all)
Boiling water to make a stiff dough
    when mixed with meal (about 2¼
    cups)
1 tablespoon butter

Mix ingredients well. Drop from spoon into hot deep fat until brown. Drain on paper towels.

Hush Puppies must be made on the spot! Don't ever make them too far ahead because they will taste greasy.

Cabbage Slaw
Serves 10 or 12

1 large cabbage
1 red bell pepper
3 carrots
1 large onion
1 cup vinegar
1 tablespoon dry mustard
1 tablespoon sugar
1 tablespoon salt
¾ cup vegetable oil

Grate cabbage, pepper, carrots and onion. Mix vinegar, mustard, sugar and salt. Let come to boil, take from flame, add oil. Let come to boil again. Pour over cabbage, onion and sugar. Set in refrigerator. Do not mix until ready to serve.

La Fonda Pudding
Serves 8

4 eggs, separated
¾ cup sugar
1 cup finely crushed graham
    crackers
½ cup walnuts, chopped
1 teaspoon baking powder
⅛ teaspoon salt
1 teaspoon vanilla

Beat egg yolks until light. Gradually beat in sugar and continue to beat until thick. Fold in graham crackers, nuts, baking powder, salt and vanilla. Beat egg whites until stiff. Gradually beat in ¼ cup sugar to make a thick, glossy meringue. Add half meringue to egg yolk mixture and beat until well blended. Add remaining meringue and fold in lightly. Butter an 8×8-inch cake pan. Pour batter into pan and bake at 350° 45 minutes. Cool in pan 10 minutes and turn out of pan. Cut into squares and serve warm topped with whipped cream and additional chopped walnuts, if you wish.

Herbert was so pleased with the natural landscaping work done by Bob Shaheen and Curt Goodfellow that he gave them a lot on the western side of the island overlooking the lake in exchange for their work. They built what became the most–photographed house on the island, "Stoneflower," designed by Fay Jones, a well-known architect at the University of Arkansas. It's a wonderful contemporary house with a cathedral–like living room and sleeping loft (reached by ladder) and a cave–like den and bathroom below. The shower is a waterfall over the rocks. Grandchildren of mine once confessed to having climbed the rock exterior in order to glimpse bathers through the skylight. Above is a long deck overlooking the lake with two great cooking grills where they entertained many people, including *Life* photographers, with this dramatic steak recipe, which happened to be a favorite of Justice William O. Douglas.

MENU

William O. Douglas' Wood–Smoke Steak
Mushroom Eggplant Casserole
Large Tossed Salad
Orange Pecan Pie

William O. Douglas' Wood–Smoke Steak
Serves 8 to 10

Salt
Olive oil or vegetable oil
1 porterhouse steak 2½ inches thick
1 bottle Worcestershire sauce
¼ pound butter
3 cloves garlic
Juice of 1 lemon
1 pint tomato purée

Rub salt freely on both sides of steak, dip in oil and place directly on the coals. (A thick bed of coals is required, preferably of charcoal, but the coals of apple wood, oak or hickory will do.) Sear each side quickly. Baste with sauce made from ingredients above. Turn steak frequently, basting on each turn.

This steak has the aroma of the woods in it. It will be black and charred on the edges and will carry a delicate trace of wood smoke. To serve, cut thin slices on the diagonal.

Mushroom Eggplant Casserole
Serves 8 to 10

3 eggplants, peeled and cubed
1 cup yellow onion, finely minced
1 ½ tablespoons olive oil
1 pound fresh mushrooms, minced finely
3 tablespoons butter
Salt and pepper to taste
4 ½ ounces cream cheese
4 tablespoons parsley, minced
1 ½ teaspoons basil, minced

TOPPING:
3 tablespoons Swiss cheese, grated
3 tablespoons bread crumbs, finely minced (We use homemade rolls)
2 to 3 tablespoons melted butter

Soak eggplant in salted ice water 1 hour. Pour off water and boil in clear water until tender. Drain into colander and put into 3-quart mixing bowl.

Sauté onions slowly in skillet with olive oil until tender but not brown. Season lightly and add to eggplant in bowl.

Twist mushrooms in a cloth to wring out juice. Sauté in olive oil until lightly brown, 5 to 6 minutes. Add to bowl.

Beat cream cheese with seasonings and add to bowl. Mix well. Pour into greased casserole dish.

Sprinkle mixture of cheese and bread crumbs over top and sprinkle that with melted butter.

Place casserole in a hot water bath about ⅛ inch deep and bake in preheated 375° oven about 20 to 30 minutes until hot clear through and brown on top.

The *Mushroom Eggplant Casserole* is one of our most–requested recipes. The homemade roll topping adds to the flavor!

Orange Pecan Pie
Serves 6

1 cup white corn syrup
1 tablespoon orange juice
4 tablespoons butter, melted
4 tablespoons sugar
1 cup pecans, broken
½ teaspoon salt
1 tablespoon orange rind, grated
3 eggs

Mix well corn syrup, melted butter, sugar, nutmeats, salt, orange juice and grated orange rind. Add to the above mixture eggs which have been lightly beaten, and pour the mixture into an unbaked crust. Bake in a moderate oven 350° until well browned—about 45 minutes.

The orange tang cuts the rich sweetness of pecan pie.

"Dress for Dinner" at the Inn

Lunch is a relaxed time at the Red Apple Inn. Dinner, on the other hand, is more formal. The guests have always expected to dress for dinner, which meant a coat and tie for the men. Herbert Thomas felt strongly that people should know when they came for dinner at the Red Apple that the other guests would be dressed appropriately to contribute to the ambience required to enjoy a fine meal. The rule was unbending. More than a few people can tell stories of the trauma caused by a forgotten tie or coat. One man wore his wife's pants when he realized he had arrived for the weekend with only golf shorts. In recent years, since meals are not served by the pool, a dining room in the Inn has been set aside for casual diners.

The Red Apple Inn has been selected as the Most Romantic Restaurant in Arkansas by the *Arkansas Times* and at night it has an atmosphere of elegant informality that is romantic. I think that is partly because of the natural beauty of the setting in the treetops overlooking the lake, and also because of some of the little touches that make it special, such as the dress rule, the roses on the tables, the soufflés and the friendly but subdued service of the waiters and waitresses.

I must say that Herbert was a tyrant when it came to attention to details. He wanted everything to be perfect for the guests, but to look as natural as possible. Each tropicana rose was to face the guest when he or she arrived in the dining room, which meant an inspection before every meal. But the guests just noticed the effect, not the effort.

I wanted food that people would remember and come back for over and over again. That meant that consistency was critical. Every time a dish was cooked, it had to look and taste the same. The guests dress for dinner. Our challenge in the kitchen is to live up the anticipation of our guests. Fortunately, in our own kitchens we can be a little more spontaneous.

A brochure advertising the Red Apple describes the food this way: "four-star cuisine that is somewhere between caviar and spoon bread; but, of course, we have them both. A touch of France, a lot of the South result in gourmet dining—soufflés, homemade rolls and incredible desserts!"

Dancing has always been popular entertainment at the Red Apple Inn, especially on Saturday night when there is always live music night at the Inn. Many local bands have played there, playing piano in the bar early and late and dance music in the dining room during dinner. But the group, *Morning Side,* has been the band of choice for fifteen years, and their fans come back just to dance to their music.

Sometimes the entertainment at dinner is spontaneous. The raccoons like to entertain the guests by playing on the deck outside the windows—especially when they know they might be rewarded with leftover rolls or popcorn.

Occasionally the weather presents a more dramatic kind of show. Dr. Mickey Barnett tells of many nights when a storm has lit up the sky with thousands of lightning flashes reflected in the lake and the crash of thunder echoing from the hills. During especially violent displays, dinner service stops and the employees and guests experience nature's dramatic theater from the security of their indoor seats high above the lake.

Here are just a few of the menus offered for the selection of the guests. Some are quite simple and others more sophisticated. Every dinner starts, like lunch, with an iced assortment of crunchies. After the entree is served, a vegetable or cheese soufflé on a silver dish is passed by the waiter. All are popular and are easily duplicated at home. Our famous homemade hot rolls accompany all the dinners unless a different bread is appropriate. Feel free to mix and match the recipes—after you've tried ours! I'm sure you can come up with some wonderful variations!

MENU

Chicken Breast Eden Isle
Fluffy Arkansas Steamed Rice
Spinach Soufflé
Caesar Salad
Jean's Famous Rolls
Red Apple Apple Pie

Chicken Breast Eden Isle

Serves 6

6 chicken breasts, halved, boned and skinned
6 slices bacon
1 package dried beef
2 cans cream of chicken soup
1½ cups sour cream
1 package cream cheese
Pepper to taste

Pepper, do NOT salt chicken breasts. Wrap one slice bacon around each breast. Place layer of dried beef in bottom of baking dish. Place bacon–wrapped breasts in dish. Mix together chicken soup, sour cream and cream cheese in mixer or food processor. Cover chicken breasts with mixture. and cover baking dish tightly with foil. Place in 325° oven 2 hours. When tender, remove foil and let brown well. Serve on a bed of rice.

This is a recipe I devised when I was first preparing menus for the Inn. We wanted to stress Arkansas products where possible. It has stayed on the menu more than 20 years because of its popularity, and we still get requests for the recipe.

Fluffy Arkansas Steamed Rice

Serves 8

5 quarts water
1 teaspoon salt
2 cups long grain rice

Bring water and salt to boil in a large saucepan. Sprinkle in rice and cook, covered, over moderately high heat 18 minutes. Drain the rice in a large colander and rinse under running water. Put the colander over a pan of boiling water and steam the rice, covered with a tea towel and the lid, 20 to 30 minutes, or until it is fluffy and dry. Transfer to a heated serving dish.

Spinach Soufflé
Serves 4 to 6

3 tablespoons butter
3 tablespoons flour
1 cup boiling milk
¼ cup mayonnaise
4 egg yolks
¾ cup chopped, cooked spinach
½ teaspoon salt
¼ teaspoon nutmeg
⅛ teaspoon pepper
1 tablespoon green onions, minced
1 tablespoon butter
5 egg whites
Pinch of salt
¼ teaspoon cream of tartar

Melt butter in saucepan. Stir in flour and cook over moderate heat 2 minutes. Remove from heat. When mixture has stopped bubbling pour into it the boiling milk. Beat vigorously until well blended. Return to fire and boil 1 minute, stirring. Sauce will be thick. Remove from heat. Add mayonnaise. Beat the egg yolks. Drop them into hot cream sauce and beat.

Blend spinach in a food processor or blender. Add salt, nutmeg and pepper. Sauté green onion in 1 tablespoon butter until tender. Add to spinach in blender. Now add this to cream sauce and thoroughly mix with wooden spoon. Beat the egg whites with the pinch of salt and cream of tarter added until stiff. Stir ¼ of the egg whites into spinach–cream sauce mixture. Fold in the rest of the egg whites (gently) and turn mixture into buttered 6-cup soufflé dish. Set in a water bath on middle rack in oven preheated to 350°. Bake 25 to 30 minutes or until firm.

Caesar Salad
Serves 6

2 heads Romaine lettuce
1 clove garlic, peeled
1 cup olive oil
4 slices stale bread
Dash of cayenne pepper
Dash of Tabasco sauce
½ teaspoon sugar
6 anchovy filets, diced and mashed
1 egg
Juice of 1 lemon
⅜ cup Parmesan cheese, freshly grated

Tear off leaves from lettuce. Wash well and dry thoroughly, being careful not to bruise leaves. Put in refrigerator to chill. Crush garlic and let stand overnight in olive oil. Keep in refrigerator.

Trim crusts from bread. Cut into cubes and brown these croutons in about ¼ cup of the olive oil, which has been strained to remove garlic. Sauté over moderate heat, turning croutons to brown on all sides. Drain on paper towels and set aside.

In a jar add to the garlic–flavored salad oil: pepper, Tabasco, sugar and anchovy filets.

Break chilled romaine leaves in pieces and place in large bowl. Sprinkle with freshly ground pepper and salt. Pour over the seasoned olive oil and mix thoroughly so that every leaf is well coated and shiny.

Boil egg 1 minute. Remove, crack shell and drip into salad. Squeeze the juice of 1 large lemon (about 3 tablespoons) over egg and stir gently into salad. It will have a creamy appearance. Taste for seasoning.

When just ready to serve, sprinkle Parmesan cheese and the croutons over salad. Toss lightly to mix. We like to serve this with French bread slashed into slices, spread with garlic butter and heated in the oven.

Jean's Famous Rolls
Makes about 16 to 18 rolls

½ cup butter
⅓ cup sugar
1 teaspoon salt
½ cup boiling water
1 ¼ tablespoons dry yeast
½ cup lukewarm water
1 egg
3 cups flour
Melted butter
Garlic powder
Sesame seeds

Pour ½ cup boiling water over the butter, sugar and salt in a large bowl. Let cool. Dissolve the yeast in ½ cup lukewarm water and beat in the eggs. Add to the cooled mixture. Add the flour, 1 cup at a time, beating after each addition. Cover the bowl and let sit overnight in refrigerator. Take out 2 hours before baking. Roll out on a lightly floured board. Cut in rounds; crease with a knife and fold over. Place close together in a buttered baking pan and brush tops with melted butter. Sprinkle a few grains of garlic powder on top and then sprinkle with sesame seeds. Bake in a 425° oven about 12 to 15 minutes or until well browned.

Red Apple Apple Pie

PASTRY:

2 cups unbleached white flour
½ teaspoon salt
⅓ cup vegetable shortening
⅓ cup butter
Ice water (about ⅓ cup)

Have all materials ice cold. Sift flour and salt into a bowl. Cut in the shortening and butter until shortening is evenly mixed in bits no larger than peas. Add ice water to hold the dough together. Pat gently into a ball, wrap in plastic wrap and chill thoroughly.

Turn out on a smooth cold board. Cut with knife into a square ball, then flatten with the rolling pin. Roll in an oblong shape ½ inch thick. Fold in thirds and roll again, repeat and after third rolling, roll into round shape to fit the pie pan. Return to refrigerator for ½ hour. Makes two 9-inch pie shells or 1 double crust pie.

FILLING:

1 ½ cups sugar
½ teaspoon cinnamon
Juice of 1 orange
Grated rind of 1 orange
Juice of 1 lemon
5 tablespoons butter
6 tart apples, peeled and sliced

Mix all ingredients except apples in saucepan and bring to a boil. Place layer of apples in pan lined with uncooked pastry. Pour some of the mixture over apples, continue layers until pan is rounded. Place thin strips of pastry in latticework pattern on top. Brush with cream and bake at 325° until brown. Turn temperature down to 300° and bake until done, about 30 minutes longer.

An old friend, Mary Shepherd, served this apple pie many years ago. When we were looking for the "right" recipe for our apple pie, I thought of this recipe. It's light and tangy.

Rainbow trout is a special feature at the Inn because of the famous trout fishing on the Little Red River below the dam. Many people have fond memories of foggy mornings on the Little Red before the first release of cold water when the trout would start to bite. Usually before noon the limit was caught, and the guide would clean and package the catch after recording the picture of the days' catch on film.

Often guests ask us to prepare trout they have caught that morning. We would usually prepare the *Trout Amandine* that follows or the *Broiled Trout with Cucumber Sauce.* Usually we serve trout that were raised commercially—both are delicious and easy to prepare.

MENU

Trout Amandine
Emerald Rice
Hearts of Palm Salad
Cream Cheese Soufflé
Hot Rolls
Crème Brulée

Trout Amandine
Serves 6

6 fresh trout, cleaned
¼ cup flour
1 teaspoon salt
¼ teaspoon cayenne pepper
1 cup butter
1 cup sliced almonds
1 tablespoon lemon juice
Lemon wedges
Fresh parsley, chopped

Combine flour, salt and pepper; coat trout well on both sides. Sauté 3 trout in a 12-inch skillet over medium heat 5 minutes on each side, using ¼ cup butter for each batch. Remove to heated platter and cover to keep warm. When all fish are cooked, discard butter and wipe out the skillet. Add remaining butter and almonds to skillet; cook over low heat, stirring frequently, until almonds become pale golden color. Remove from heat and stir in lemon juice. Pour almonds over cooked trout. Serve immediately with lemon wedges and chopped parsley.

Emerald Rice

Serves 10

4 eggs, separated
4 cups cooked rice
1 cup raw spinach, minced
½ cup green pepper, minced
¼ cup onion, minced
1 cup heavy cream, whipped
⅓ cup Parmesan cheese
1 teaspoon paprika
1 teaspoon salt
1 cup sour cream
3 tablespoons chives, minced

Beat egg yolks. Add rice, spinach, green pepper, onion, whipped cream, paprika, cheese and salt. Fold in stiffly beaten egg whites. Pour into buttered ring mold, set in pan of water. Bake 45 to 55 minutes at 350° or until set. Serve sour cream and chives on the side.

Emerald Rice is much like a soufflé. It is a good way to use leftover rice.

Hearts of Palm Salad

Serves 1

3 Boston or Bibb lettuce leaves
3 sprigs watercress
3 whole pieces heart of palm, sliced
　　lengthwise
3 thin slices sweet red pepper
2 tablespoons *Vinaigrette Dressing*

Place sliced palm stalks on bed of lettuce, garnish with red pepper and dressing.

Cream Cheese Soufflé
Serves 4 to 6

4 eggs, separated
¼ teaspoon salt
1 teaspoon flour
6 ounces cream cheese
1 cup sour cream
¼ cup honey

Beat yolks of eggs until thick and creamy. Add salt and flour. Combine sour cream and cream cheese, blend until smooth. Add to egg yolks, beat with electric beater until smooth, adding honey gradually. Beat egg whites until stiff but not dry, and fold in yolk mixture. Pour into ungreased 1½-quart soufflé dish. Place in pan of water and bake in preheated 300° oven 1 hour.

This unusual soufflé has been served with dinner every Saturday night since the Red Apple opened. Many people have requested the recipe and it has appeared in the *Arkansas Gazette* several times.

Crème Brulée
Serves 6

3 cups heavy cream
⅓ cup sugar
6 egg yolks
1 vanilla bean, split
½ cup light brown sugar

Pour the cream into a heavy saucepan and place over low heat. Add the granulated sugar and heat, stirring constantly, until the sugar dissolves and the cream is hot. Do not allow it to boil. Beat the yolks with a rotary or electric beater until light in color. Add the hot cream very slowly, stirring constantly with a wooden spatula. Do not beat. Stir in the vanilla. Strain into a greased 1-quart baking dish. Place the dish in a pan of hot water to the depth of about an inch. Bake in a preheated 300° oven until a knife inserted in the center comes out clean—about 45 minutes. Remove from oven and allow to stand at room temperature until cool. Chill in the refrigerator.

Several hours before serving, sift the brown sugar over the top of the custard. Set the baking dish in a bed of cracked ice and place in a preheated broiler just long enough for the sugar to melt. Watch sharply to see that the sugar doesn't burn. Best not to even close the oven door. Chill and serve cold.

MENU

Braised Lamb Shanks
Steamed Barley
Asparagus Salad Mold
French Bread with Butter and Dill
Bread Pudding with Orange Sauce

Braised Lamb Shanks
Serves 6 to 8

4 tablespoons butter
1½ cups onions, finely chopped
½ cup celery, finely chopped
½ cup carrots, finely chopped
1 teaspoon garlic, finely chopped
6 to 7 pounds lamb shank or shin, sawed into 8 pieces, each 2½ inches long and tied with string around their circumferences
Salt to taste
Freshly ground black pepper
½ cup flour
½ cup olive oil
1 cup dry white wine
¾ cup beef or chicken stock
½ teaspoon dried basil
½ teaspoon dried thyme
3 cups whole tomatoes, drained and chopped
6 parsley sprigs
2 bay leaves

GREMOLATA:
1 tablespoon lemon peel, grated
1 teaspoon garlic, finely chopped
3 tablespoons parsley, finely chopped

In a Dutch oven that has a tight cover and is large enough to snugly hold the pieces of lamb standing up in one layer, melt the butter over moderate heat. Add onions, carrots, celery and garlic. Cook, stirring occasionally, until soft. Remove from heat.

Season lamb with salt and pepper, roll in flour and shake off excess. In a heavy skillet heat 6 tablespoons olive oil until haze forms. Brown lamb in the oil over moderately high heat, 4 or 5 pieces at a time, adding more oil as needed. Transfer browned pieces to the casserole and stand them side by side on top of the vegetables.

Preheat oven to 350°. Discard almost all of the fat from the skillet. Pour in the wine and boil briskly over high heat until it is reduced to about ½ cup. Scrape in any browned bits clinging to the pan. Stir in the stock, basil, thyme, tomatoes, parsley and bay leaves and bring to a boil. Pour it all over the lamb. If it does not come halfway up the side of the lamb, add a little more stock. Bring the casserole to a boil on top of the stove, cover and bake in the lower third of the oven about 1 hour and 15 minutes until tender.

To serve, arrange the lamb on a heated platter and spoon the sauce and vegetables from the casserole around them. Sprinkle the top with the *Gremolata*.

For a more elegant version, remove the casserole from the oven when the meat is tender and increase the oven temperature to 450°. With tongs, carefully transfer the lamb to a large oven-proof platter, being careful not to lose the marrow in the bones on the way. Place the platter in the top third of the oven and bake the lamb 5 to 10 minutes, or until it is deep brown and brightly glazed.

Meanwhile, strain the contents of the casserole through a sieve into a 2– to 3-quart saucepan. Boil the liquid over high heat, stirring, until it has reduced to about half. Taste and season more highly if needed. Serve the sauce over the glazed lamb and sprinkle the top with *Gremolata*.

Lamb always reminds me of Ireland. One year when our daughters had returned home from a visit with us in Waterville, Herbert wrote them, "With the purse getting flatter, our menu is now sardines and crackers for lunch and sheep's shanks for dinner." He was looking for their sympathy, but he actually loved the simple Irish cooking.

Steamed Barley
Serves 6

½ cup onion, chopped
2 cloves garlic, mashed
1 tablespoon butter
1 cup fresh mushrooms, sliced
1½ cups barley
1 tablespoon parsley, chopped
½ teaspoon dried thyme
½ teaspoon dried marjoram
Salt and pepper to taste
2 cups chicken or beef bouillon
Optional: ½ cup pecans, chopped

Sauté onions and garlic in butter until soft. Transfer to a lightly buttered casserole dish. Add mushrooms, barley and seasonings. Pour bouillon over all and bake in 350° oven about 30 minutes or until barley is tender. Add liquid if dish becomes too dry. Serve hot.

Asparagus Salad Mold
Serves 12

2 tablespoons unflavored gelatin
½ cup cold water
3 cups chicken or beef consommé
8 strips crisp bacon, crumbled
3 small cans green asparagus tips
¼ cup toasted slivered almonds
Mayonnaise seasoned with peach
 or mango chutney
1 tablespoon lemon juice

Soften gelatin in cold water. Dissolve over hot water. Add to consommé and mix well. Drain asparagus well and place in oiled mold, sprinkling each layer with bacon and almonds. Cover with gelatin mixture. Chill till firm. Serve on lettuce with mayonnaise seasoned with juice from chutney.

Bread Pudding

Serves 6 to 8

2 cups bread crumbs
1 quart milk
4 eggs, separated
1 cup sugar
1 lemon rind, grated
¼ cup almonds, chopped
Butter
Brown sugar, sifted

Soak bread crumbs in milk ½ hour. Beat egg yolks well with sugar, add soaked crumbs, lemon rind, almonds and fold in beaten egg whites. Place in individual molds, generously greased with butter, and sprinkled with brown sugar. Bake in 350° oven ½ hour or until firm. Remove to dessert plates and serve with *Orange Sauce.*

ORANGE SAUCE:
Juice of 2 oranges
¼ cup sugar
Grated rind of ½ lemon
Grated rind of ½ orange
½ cup water

Boil all together 3 minutes and serve over bread pudding.

MENU

Beef Brisket with Kraut
Creamy Mashed Potatoes
Stewed Apples
Hot Buttered Rye Bread
Red Apple Chess Pie

Beef Brisket with Kraut
Serves 6 to 8

4 pounds short ribs or 2 pounds boneless beef brisket
1 large onion, coarsley chopped
1 quart sauerkraut, chopped
1 large potato, grated
1 tablespoon caraway seeds
1 teaspoon boveril
½ cup sour cream

Put beef brisket on burner in covered container with enough water to barely cover. Simmer slowly until meat is tender enough to fall from the bones and the water is reduced to about 4 cups. (Salt lightly—not too much as the kraut is salty.)

About 30 minutes before serving time add sauerkraut. Grate 1 large raw potato into the kraut (this thickens gravy) and add caraway seeds and boveril. Just before serving, add sour cream. Serve on mound of fluffy creamed potatoes. (Use your own favorite recipe—with plenty of butter and cream!)

Sauerkraut is often a Saturday night special—for a more casual meal. I learned to make it from my German Swiss forebears and my family loves it—especially on a winter's night. Beer goes well with this.

Red Apple Chess Pie
Serves 6

1 unbaked 9-inch pie shell
2 cups brown sugar
1 tablespoon flour
½ teaspoon nutmeg
1 cup cream
4 eggs, slightly beaten
1 teaspoon lemon juice
½ teaspoon lemon rind, grated
½ cup melted margarine

Sift sugar with flour and nutmeg. Add the rest of the ingredients one at a time, stirring continuously. Pour into pie shell. Bake at 375° 45 minutes. Cool and serve with whipped cream.

MENU

Mushroom-Filled Meat Loaf with Sour Cream Sauce
Green Beans
Cole Slaw Mold
Chocolate Roll

Mushroom-Filled Meat Loaf with Sour Cream Sauce
Serves 8

1 cup fresh mushrooms, sliced
½ cup onion, chopped
1 tablespoon butter
1 cup sour cream
1 large egg
¼ cup milk
¾ pound ground beef
⅓ cup bread crumbs
1 teaspoon salt
¼ teaspoon black pepper
1 teaspoon Worcestershire sauce

Sauté mushrooms and onion in butter. Remove from heat and stir in sour cream. Set aside. Preheat the oven to 350°. Combine remaining ingredients in a separate bowl, and put half of the mixture into a 9×5-inch loaf pan. Make shallow trough down the center of the meat for filling. Spoon sour cream–mushroom mixture into this indention. Shape the rest of the meat over the filling, making sure all filling is covered. Seal meat loaf well around the edges.

Bake 1 hour. Let stand 15 minutes before slicing. Garnish top with remaining fresh mushrooms, thinly sliced and sautéed.

SOUR CREAM SAUCE:
½ cup sour cream
½ teaspoon Dijon mustard
½ teaspoon prepared horseradish
¼ teaspoon salt
Dash each, nutmeg and white
   pepper

Stir together in small saucepan over low heat. Serve hot with the meat loaf.

This meat loaf recipe is a little more "dressy" than the usual. My niece, Margaret Hastings, shared this recipe with me.

Green Beans

Serves 6

1 pound green beans
Leftover ham or salt meat
Salt and pepper to taste
Dash of sugar
Garlic, minced
Herbs to taste
Optional: bacon drippings

I recommend fresh Kentucky Wonders, entirely freed of string. Cook in small amount of water with a piece of ham or salt meat. Season to taste. A bit of bacon drippings may be added. Southerners cook these beans a long time, so the flavors are well blended and the beans wilted. You may prefer a shorter cooking time, leaving the beans greener and crisper.

Cole Slaw Mold

Serves 8

1 package lemon jello
1 envelope plain gelatin
1 small can crushed pineapple
1 cup green cabbage, shredded
½ green pepper, chopped
¼ cup mayonnaise
1 cup sour cream
1 tablespoon sugar
1 teaspoon salt

Mix jello and gelatin with proper amount of pineapple juice and water according to directions. Let cool and when slightly thickened, stir in the other ingredients. Pour into lightly greased mold and chill until firm.

Chocolate Roll
Serves 6 to 8

5 eggs, separated
1 cup powdered sugar
Whipped cream
3 tablespoons cocoa

Beat egg yolks until thick, add sugar and beat thoroughly. Add cocoa, fold in stiffly beaten whites. Spread in buttered and floured 9×13-inch pan and bake about 20 minutes in oven at 350°. Turn out on floured cloth. Cover with damp cloth. Cool, spread with whipped cream. Roll and cut into slices. Serve with *Chocolate Sauce.*

CHOCOLATE SAUCE:
4 ounces dark sweet chocolate
½ ounce bitter chocolate
3 tablespoons liquid coffee
1 cup light cream
½ cup sugar
1 teaspoon vanilla extract
1 teaspoon cornstarch
4 egg yolks
½ cup heavy cream, whipped

Melt chocolate with coffee in double boiler. Scald cream with vanilla and sugar. Stir until mixture comes to a boil. Mix corn starch with egg yolks in a saucepan. Strain hot cream into egg yolks. Add chocolate mixture and cook slowly, stirring, until mixture coats spoon. Strain, chill in refrigerator and fold in whipped cream. Serve with *Chocolate Roll* or with *Cold Orange Soufflé.*

A wonderful old–fashioned southern cook, Flora Raney, made a *Chocolate Roll* and brought it to my family. We liked it so well, she shared the recipe.

Festive Occasions in the Gate Room

The Spanish wrought iron gate leading to the "After Five" room and into the Gate Room gives that part of the Inn an aura of history and romance and hints of a special evening in the room beyond. Bridal parties, family celebrations, business dinners, holiday meals all have been enjoyed in the elegant, raftered dining room decorated with red fabric walls and Spanish antiques. Heavy oak tables (hand made by a local woodworker) and black and white Staffordshire china add to the feeling of elegance.

The gate has an interesting history. It was made in 1505 by Spanish craftsmen for use in the palace of the Governor of Sevilla Province. Many years later, in 1754, fire destroyed the ceiling of the palace. King Charles of Spain had the ceiling repaired, and the palace was converted into a Court of Justice for use until the end of the Spanish Civil War. In 1939, the city of Sevilla decided to rent the palace. It was divided into eight apartments of twelve rooms each. In 1965 the city had the palace dismantled to make use of the valuable land on which the palace stood. The lovely 460-year old gate became available for purchase.

The gate became a part of the Inn as a happy accident back in the early 1960s when the Inn was being built. The story goes that Herbert dispatched Mr. Mouso to Spain to oversee the manufacture of furnishings for the guest rooms and public rooms of the Inn. While in Sevilla, Mr. Mouso discovered "the gate" in a building that was being torn down—a rare occurrence in Europe. The gate was so beautiful, he cabled Herbert, telling him what a magnificent art object it was, and asking his permission to buy it. Without knowing the price, cost of shipping, or the dimensions, Herbert granted permission by cable. When the gate arrived, the roof was in place and the gate was too tall for the space. The problem was solved by excavating the floor and installing it in front of the circular steps leading up to the dining room. The gate has since been moved to the entrance to the "After Five" room, which leads into the Gate Room. Visitors have since enjoyed its touch of European elegance.

Islanders and Country Club members like to entertain their friends in the Gate

Room. For large crowds, the cocktail buffet is the preferred form of entertaining. Here we present some of the special hors d'oeuvres and party dishes.

COCKTAIL BUFFET FOR A CROWD

Salted Pecans with Rosemary
Oysters Broiled in Bacon
Hot Crab Meat Dip
Sliced Beef Tenderloin
Cheese Ball with Pecans
Smoked Salmon
Tiny-Sliced Rye Bread
Marinated Tomatoes
Smoked Oyster Dip with Crudités
Mushrooms Stuffed with Spinach
Caviar Mousse

Salted Pecans with Rosemary

1 pound pecan halves
¼ pound unsalted butter
½ teaspoon sugar
½ teaspoon rosemary, crushed
1 teaspoon salt

Toast pecan halves 20 minutes in 250° oven. Mix sugar, butter and rosemary and melt together. Mix with toasted pecans, coating all the nut meats. Add salt. Toast another 60 minutes until butter has been absorbed and pecans are crisp. Pecans will keep for several weeks in tightly covered tin box.

Oysters Broiled in Bacon

12 raw oysters
6 slices bacon

Wrap one half of a bacon slice around each oyster and skewer with a toothpick. Broil in oven until bacon is cooked. Keep warm while serving.

Hot Crab Meat Dip

8 ounces cream cheese, softened
3 tablespoons minced onion
6 ounces lump crab meat
1 tablespoon sherry
1 teaspoon horseradish
¼ teaspoon salt
4 or 5 drops Tabasco sauce

Mix and bake at 350° 15 to 20 minutes. Serve hot with crackers or chips.

Sliced Beef Tenderloin
Serves about 20

5 pounds beef tenderloin

MARINADE:
1 8-ounce bottle soy sauce
1 cup olive oil
1 cup wine vinegar
Salt and pepper to taste
4 tablespoons boveril
2 cloves garlic, crushed
2 tablespoons Worcestershire
    sauce

Select the best beef available. Marinate tenderloin in marinade 2 to 3 hours before baking. Bake in hot oven (450°) or on a charcoal grill 20 to 30 minutes or until brown on the outside and very rare inside (110° on meat thermometer). Let stand at room temperature and slice on the diagonal.

Blend and let stand overnight.

Cheese Ball with Pecans

16 ounces cream cheese, softened
8 ounces sharp cheddar cheese
1 tablespoon scraped onion
Dash cayenne pepper
Dash salt
1 tablespoon red bell pepper,
    chopped
1 tablespoon green pepper,
    chopped
1 teaspoon lemon juice
2 teaspoons Worcestershire sauce
½ cup pecans, chopped

Chop pecans in food processor and set aside. Blend remaining ingredients together and roll into a ball and cover with plastic wrap. Place in refrigerator to chill. Before serving, roll in chopped pecans and sprinkle with paprika. Serve with crackers. A variety of cheeses may be substituted. This is a good way to use small scraps of leftover cheese.

Marinated Tomatoes
Serves about 18

6 cups cherry tomatoes, halved
1 cup ripe olives, chopped
2 cups scallions, chopped
¼ cup parsley, chopped
1 teaspoon salt
2 teaspoons sugar
⅛ teaspoon turmeric
¾ teaspoon cumin
¼ teaspoon pepper
6 tablespoons olive oil
4 tablespoons lemon juice

Mix tomatoes, olives, scallion and parsley. Make a marinade with remaining ingredients and marinate at least 2 hours. Chill and serve.

My daughter, Jane McGehee, entertains often and loves to serve *Marinated Tomatoes* as a light contrast to the richer fare at a cocktail table.

Smoked Oyster Dip

1 package cream cheese, softened
1 can smoked oysters
2 tablespoons mayonnaise
1 tablespoon sherry
Dash of onion juice
Paprika
1 tablespoon chives, minced

Combine all ingredients except chives and blend in food processor. Transfer to serving bowl and garnish with paprika and chives. Serve with crisp, thinly sliced raw vegetables.

Mushrooms Stuffed with Spinach

2 pounds fresh mushrooms
2 packages frozen chopped
   spinach, thawed
2 tablespoons grated onion
1 cup buttered bread crumbs
2 tablespoons mayonnaise
¼ teaspoon cayenne pepper
¼ teaspoon nutmeg
¼ teaspoon oregano
Salt to taste
2 well beaten eggs
Dash Worcestershire sauce
Parmesan cheese, freshly grated
Optional: 5 ounces lump crab meat

Wipe mushrooms with a soft brush to clean. Remove stems and chop into bowl. Set aside mushroom caps. Squeeze water out of spinach. Mix remaining ingredients except for cheese and stuff mushrooms with mixture. Bake on cookie sheet in 350° oven until almost done. Sprinkle Parmesan cheese on top and brown under the broiler. Serve warm.

Crab meat is a nice addition to the spinach stuffing.

Caviar Mousse

5 hard-boiled eggs, chopped
3 tablespoons onion, finely
   chopped
1 cup mayonnaise
1 ½ teaspoons Worcestershire
   sauce
2 tablespoons lemon juice
¼ teaspoon Tabasco sauce
½ cup sour cream
1 teaspoon dried dill, or 10 sprigs
   fresh dill
1 package unflavored gelatin
¼ cup cold water
4 ounces lumpfish caviar

At least 3 hours before serving, lightly oil a pint-size mold and refrigerate. Combine all ingredients except gelatin, water and caviar; mix well. Soften gelatin in water and heat to dissolve. Add to rest of ingredients and fold in caviar. Pour into mold and refrigerate until set.

A special family friend, Jeane Hamilton, brought a caviar mousse to a family gathering several years ago. We all liked it so well, she shared the recipe, and it has been a part of our party menu ever since.

The Gate Room is also a place for family and company dinners. Here are some menus that have been popular.

DINNERS IN THE GATE ROOM

Mulligatawny Soup
Hot Crackers
Roast Prime Rib of Beef
Horseradish Cream Sauce
Spoonbread
Peppers Sauté
Lettuce Salad with Walnut Dressing
Chocolate Soufflé with Crème Fresche

Mulligatawny Soup
Serves about 10

6-pound chicken, cut in pieces
4 quarts cold water
1 tablespoon flour
1½ teaspoon curry powder
2 cloves
2 tart apples, sliced
1 cup tomatoes, peeled and seeded
1 green pepper, chopped
½ cup onion, chopped
½ cup celery chopped
½ cup carrots, chopped
1 teaspoon chopped parsley
⅛ teaspoon mace
1 teaspoon sugar
Salt and pepper
¼ cup butter

Sauté vegetables and chicken in butter until brown. Add flour, curry powder and cloves. Stir and add rest of ingredients. Cook slowly until chicken is tender. Remove chicken, cool, debone and cut meat in small pieces. Place the rest of soup in blender or food processor and purée until smooth. Add chicken to soup and serve hot.

Hot Crackers

Saltine crackers
Butter
Paprika

Spread crackers lightly with butter and sprinkle with paprika. Toast in a 350° oven and serve hot.

Roast Prime Rib of Beef

About 3 servings per pound

6 whole celery stalks
6 whole carrots
6 onions, halved
15-pound prime rib of beef
Salt
Crushed black pepper
2 cups fresh parsley, minced or 1
   cup parsley flakes

Place celery, carrots and onions in bottom of large roasting pan. Place roast on top and cover with the mixture of salt, pepper and parsley. Cover and bake in a slow oven (250°) 4 hours until well-done on the outside, but rare in the center. Serve thick slices with natural juices poured over.

Horseradish Cream Sauce

½ cup heavy cream
3 tablespoons mayonnaise
½ teaspoon salt
1 tablespoon tarragon vinegar
Dash cayenne pepper
1 teaspoon Dijon mustard
2 tablespoons horseradish, drained

Whip cream until thick. Fold in mayonnaise, then slowly add remaining ingredients. Serve very cold. This is particularly good with roast beef or cold cauliflower.

Spoon Bread
Serves 6

1 quart milk
2 cups white cornmeal
1 cup butter or margarine
2 teaspoons baking powder
1 teaspoon salt
6 eggs, separated

Heat milk in top of double boiler. Add cornmeal gradually, stirring constantly. Cook, stirring, until mixture becomes thick and mushy. Remove from heat. Blend in butter. Let cool slightly. Combine baking powder and salt; blend with cornmeal mixture. Beat egg yolks. Stir small amount of cornmeal mixture into yolks; combine with remaining mixture. Beat egg whites until stiff. Fold into cornmeal mixture. Pour into greased 3-quart baking dish. Set dish in a pan of hot water. Bake at 325° 60 to 70 minutes, or until firm and brown on top.

Spoon Bread is really a cornmeal soufflé—elegant Southern eating!

Peppers Sauté
Serves 4

1 clove garlic, slivered
1 medium onion, chopped
4 tablespoons olive oil
2 large green peppers, sliced thinly in long strips
2 large sweet red peppers, sliced thinly in long strips
Salt and freshly ground pepper to taste
3 large tomatoes, peeled and chopped
2 leaves fresh sweet basil (½ teaspoon dried)
Pinch coriander

Sauté garlic and onion in oil 5 minutes. Add peppers with ½ teaspoon salt and sauté gently 10 minutes. Add tomatoes and sweet basil. Cover and simmer until peppers are tender.

Lettuce Salad with Walnut Dressing
Serves 4

1 head Boston or bibb lettuce
½ red onion, thinly sliced
¼ cup walnuts, chopped

DRESSING:
1 clove garlic, minced
1 tablespoon Dijon mustard
3 tablespoons lemon juice
8 tablespoons walnut oil
Salt and freshly ground black
    pepper, to taste

Whisk together garlic, mustard and lemon juice. Slowly add oil in a steady stream. Season to taste with salt and pepper. Toss dressing with lettuce, onion and walnuts and serve on chilled plates.

Chocolate Soufflé
Serves 4

3 tablespoons butter
2 tablespoons flour
2 squares unsweetened chocolate
1 cup milk
¼ teaspoon salt
½ cup sugar
3-inch piece vanilla bean
4 egg yolks, beaten lightly
5 egg whites, beaten stiff

Melt butter in saucepan and blend well with flour. Add chocolate. Gradually add milk, stirring constantly, and mix in salt, sugar and vanilla bean. When sauce is thick and smooth, remove from fire and cool. Remove the bean, add yolks and beat well. Fold in egg whites. Butter 1-quart soufflé dish. Sprinkle with sugar and pour in batter. Set in pan of hot water. Bake in 400° oven 15 minutes and reduce heat to 375° and cook 20 to 25 minutes more. Serve hot with *Crème Fresche*.

Crème Fresche

1 cup sour cream
1½ pint whipping cream
1 3-ounce package cream cheese,
    softened
3 tablespoons powdered sugar,
    sifted
1 tablespoon Grand Marnier liqueur

Blend well in blender. Serve with soufflés.

MENU

Relish Tray
Jellied Consommé with Vegetables
Toasted Crackers
Lobster Salad
Thousand Island Dressing
Beef Wellington
Sauce Madeira
Stuffed Tomato
Broccoli Ring
Assorted Cheeses
Cherries Jubilee

Jellied Consommé with Vegetables
Serves 6 to 8

3 cups beef consommé
3 cups chicken broth
2 pounds tomatoes, coarsely
   chopped
1½ pound chicken wings
3 egg whites, lightly beaten
3 egg shells, crushed
3 tablespoons unflavored gelatin
½ cup dry white wine
2 tablespoons lemon juice
Salt and white pepper to taste
1 cup radishes, chopped
1 cup cucumber, peeled and
   seeded
¾ cup scallions, chopped
Sour cream

In a large saucepan combine the first 6 ingredients and bring to a boil. Stir and simmer the mixture 1 hour. Ladle the hot consommé into a sieve lined with a triple layer of dampened cheesecloth set over a large bowl. In a small bowl sprinkle gelatin over wine to soften. Pour gelatin and wine into hot broth and stir until dissolved. Let the consommé cool and add lemon juice, salt and pepper and chill 30 minutes or until thickened slightly. Fold in the radish, cucumber and scallions and chill until firm. Divide the consommé among chilled bowls and garnish each serving with a dollop of sour cream.

Jellied Consommé is an elegant beginning for a company dinner. It goes with candlelight and fine crystal. But it is very simple to prepare—and is almost calorieless!

Lobster Salad
Serves 6

6 slices canned pineapple
Curly lettuce
1 cup cooked lobster meat
½ cup *Thousand Island Dressing*

Place chilled pineapple slices on lettuce and spoon cold lobster meat over each slice. Top with dressing and serve.

Thousand Island Dressing

1 cup mayonnaise
2 tablespoons chili sauce
2 tablespoons sweet pickle relish
½ hard-boiled egg, chopped
1 tablespoon red pepper, chopped
2 tablespoons ripe olives, chopped
1 tablespoon grated onion

Mix in a bowl with a spoon. The proportions may vary with taste.

This salad was served to us at Horcher's Restaurant in Madrid and always gets rave reviews.

Beef Wellington
About 3 servings per pound

This is a spectacular dish that looks difficult to prepare (and is, if you let it be). Approached in its parts, it is a relatively simple dish, if you can make the pastry work. Here is how we do it at the Red Apple Inn. We will discuss the preparation of the beef, the preparation of the duxelles that bake around the meat, the preparation of the pastry and the putting all 3 together and serving the hearty dish.

The Beef

Order a whole tenderloin of beef prepared in an even cylinder about a foot long and tied at 1-inch intervals. Marinate the tenderloin 24 hours in the following sauce, which is saved for the baking later.

⅓ cup light olive or cooking oil
½ cup onions, sliced
½ cup carrots
½ cup celery stalks
¼ teaspoon each of thyme,
  marjoram and sage
1 bay leaf
3 cloves
6 peppercorns
1 teaspoon salt
1 cup dry white wine
⅓ cup cognac

Place the oil in a saucepan with vegetables and herbs. Cook until vegetables are tender. Place the tenderloin in a container that can be placed in the refrigerator. Add the cooked vegetable mixture and pour on the wine and cognac. Cover and refrigerate. Turn the meat several times. Wipe off the marinade and dry.

Rub the meat with cooking oil, place in a roasting pan and roast at 425° 25 minutes, basting every 5 minutes with cooking oil and fat from the pan. Remove and let cool ½ hour or longer. This preliminary baking stiffens the meat and allows it to hold its shape in the crust. This can be done ahead of time and the meat placed in the refrigerator. Return to room temperature before baking in pastry.

The Mushroom Duxelles

2 pounds mushrooms
2 tablespoons butter
4 tablespoons shallots or green
  onions, minced
½ cup dry Madeira wine
1 pinch salt and pepper
4 or 5 tablespoons mousse de foie
  gras

Brush mushrooms to clean and cut into small pieces. Twist them in the corner of a towel a few at a time to remove any juices. Save the juice for the Madeira sauce. Then sauté the mushrooms 7 or 8 minutes in butter with the shallots or scallions. When the pieces begin to separate, add the Madeira and boil rapidly until the liquid has evaporated. Season to taste with salt and pepper and beat in the mousse de foie gras. Refrigerate in a covered bowl. Beat to soften just before using.

The Pastry

3 cups all–purpose flour
1¾ sticks butter, chilled
4 tablespoons shortening, chilled
¾ cup ice water

Blend together and chill 2 hours before using. So that the crust will be crisp when served, it is done in 2 parts: a cooked bottom case to hold the beef, and a flaky dough topping.

PART 1.
THE BOTTOM PASTRY CASE

Butter a 12-inch cookie sheet. Roll ½ of the chilled pastry into a rectangle 16×7 inches about ⅛ inch thick. Prick the sides and bottom to keep it from puffing in the oven. Chill at least an hour. Bake until slightly browned in an oven preheated to 425° 12 to 15 minutes. Let cool 10 minutes on pan, then remold. Bottom may be refrigerated or frozen.

PART 2.
THE TOPPING

Roll the remaining dough into a 8×18-inch rectangle, spreading cold but soft butter over the bottom and folding in half to enclose the butter. Repeat with another 1½ tablespoon of butter, rolling the dough into a rectangle and folding it in thirds as though folding a letter. The pastry will be light and flaky when baked. Chill 2 hours and then roll into a 16×10-inch rectangle. Cut a strip from the long end and reserve for decorations. Lay the large rectangle on a flat baking sheet lined with waxed paper and a damp towel and refrigerate.

PART 3.
PUTTING IT ALL TOGETHER

The dish is assembled just before baking, which takes about 45 minutes. The Beef Wellington should rest about 20 minutes before carving and serving. In assembling, place the baked pastry case on a baking sheet and spread half of the mushroom mixture on the bottom of the case. Remove the trussing strings and set the beef in the case, covering the meat with the remaining mushrooms. Paint the sides of the case with egg glaze (1 egg beaten with ½ teaspoon water), and lay the pastry topping over the meat, allowing edges to fall down about 1 inch on sides of the case; press pastry onto sides of the case. Paint pastry topping with glaze, affix decorations and paint again with glaze. Make cross–hatch marking over the glaze with a knife, to give texture to the glaze when baked. Make 3 ⅛-inch vent holes centered about 3 inches apart in top of the pastry and insert paper or foil funnels for escaping steam. Plunge a meat thermometer through the central hole and into the center of the meat.

Bake 20 to 25 minutes in middle level of a preheated 425° oven or until the pastry has started to brown. Then lower oven to 375° and bake 20 to 25 minutes more, or to a meat thermometer reading of 137° for rare beef. Let rest at a temperature of not more than 120° at least 20 minutes before serving. When serving, carve as though cutting a sausage into 1-inch slices. The pastry will crumble slightly as you carve the beef; a very sharp serrated knife will minimize this.

Beef Wellington is served at very special dinners at the Inn. It is popular dish for two on Valentine's Day, along with *Rack of Lamb* and *Chateaubriand.*

Sauce Madeira

2 cups beef bouillon
12 tablespoons tomato paste
2 tablespoons cornstarch
¼ cup Madeira wine

Simmer marinade ingredients and mushroom juices with beef bouillon and 12 tablespoons tomato paste 1 hour; when reduced to 2 cups, strain, degrease, season and thicken with cornstarch beaten with Madeira wine. Serve as an accompaniment to the *Beef Wellington*.

Stuffed Tomato
Serves 6

6 firm, ripe red tomatoes
Salt and pepper
2 cloves garlic, minced
3 tablespoons shallots or green onions, minced
4 tablespoons fresh basil, minced and parsley, minced
⅛ teaspoon thyme
Salt and pepper to taste
¼ cup olive oil
½ cup fine, white, dry bread crumbs
2 tablespoons Parmesan cheese, optional

Preheat oven to 400°. Remove stems and cut tomatoes in half crosswise. Gently press out the juice and seeds. Sprinkle halves lightly with salt and pepper.

Blend all the ingredients in mixing bowl. Taste for seasoning. Fill each tomato half with the mixture and sprinkle with a few drops of olive oil. Arrange tomatoes in a roasting pan. (May be prepared ahead to this point.) Shortly before serving, place them in the upper part of oven and bake 10 to 15 minutes, or until tomatoes are tender, but hold their shapes, and filling has browned lightly.

Cut off top of tomato and make slashes across top. Season, top with butter and Parmesan cheese and broil until butter and cheese are melted.

Broccoli Ring
Serves 8

1 pint broccoli, chopped, cooked
   and drained
1 cup mayonnaise
3 tablespoons butter
3 tablespoons flour
1 cup warm milk
Salt and cayenne pepper to taste
1 teaspoon onion juice
6 well beaten eggs

Mix broccoli and mayonnaise. Make thick white sauce by stirring flour into melted butter in saucepan, adding milk and stirring until thick. Add to broccoli and mayonnaise mixture. Season to taste with salt, onion juice and pepper. Add eggs. Cook at 300° in a buttered ring mold set in a pan of water until firm (about 1 hour). Unmold and serve on platter. Pile tiny buttered beets or carrots in center for color.

Cherries Jubilee
Serves 4

1 can dark pitted cherries
1 cup sugar
¼ cup orange juice
1 tablespoon cornstarch or
   arrowroot
2 tablespoons Kirsch

Cook cherries with juice, sugar and orange juice until liquid is reduced. Thicken with a little cornstarch mixed with water. Pour Kirsch on top and flame. When flame dies down, serve over ice cream in long–stemmed glasses.

Cherries Jubilee is a quick and easy dessert, but impressive when flamed at the table.

MENU

Tomato Basil Soup
Chateaubriand with Sauce Béarnaise
Stuffed Mushrooms
Duchess Potatoes
Artichoke Bottoms
Hearts of Romaine Salad
Crème Caramel

Tomato Basil Soup
Serves 8

1 carrot, chopped
1 large stalk celery, chopped
1 leek, chopped
1 clove garlic, crushed
1 tablespoon olive oil
2 pounds fresh tomatoes, peeled,
　seeded and chopped
4 cups chicken broth
1 tablespoon fresh basil
1½ teaspoons fresh thyme
1 bay leaf
Salt and pepper to taste
Sugar to taste

Sauté carrots, celery, leeks and garlic in olive oil until vegetables are soft. Add tomatoes, chicken broth and fresh herbs. Bring to soft boil and cook covered 25 minutes. Taste for seasoning. When served as a first course, strain and serve as a broth, hot or ice cold.

Chateaubriand
Serves 4

2 1-pound slices Chateaubriand
¼ cup dry white wine
¼ cup shallots or green onions
1 tablespoon butter
1 pinch tarragon, finely chopped
1 pinch cayenne pepper
½ teaspoon lemon

The chateaubriand is taken from the thickest part of the filet of beef. Great care should be taken not to overcook the outside while the inside remains raw. Grill or broil the chateaubriand until meat thermometer inserted in the center reads 110°.

Put wine and shallots in crêpe pan and simmer 2 or 3 minutes. When slightly browned, add the meat glaze, butter and remaining seasonings. Pour over thick slices of rare meat.

Béarnaise Sauce

3 sprigs tarragon, minced
3 sprigs chervil, minced
2 shallots, finely chopped
4 crushed peppercorns
¼ cup tarragon vinegar
¼ cup white wine
3 egg yolks
1 tablespoon water
1 cup soft butter, divided into 3
   parts
Salt and cayenne pepper to taste
3 sprigs each tarragon and chervil

Combine herbs, vinegar and wine in the top of a double boiler and cook over direct heat until they are reduced to a thick paste. Cool slightly. Put the pan over hot water and cook over low heat. Add egg yolks and water. Stir briskly with a small wire whisk until the mixture is light and fluffy. Add the first portion of butter and stir constantly until thick and smooth. Add the second and third parts, stirring briskly after each addition. Season to taste with salt and cayenne. Strain it through a fine sieve, and add 3 sprigs each of tarragon and chervil, both finely chopped.

Serve *Chateaubriand* on a large wooden platter surrounded by the vegetables. The *Béarnaise Sauce* is passed at the table. This is a favorite for Valentine dinners and for anniversaries.

Stuffed Mushrooms

1 pound fresh mushrooms
2 tablespoons butter
6 green onions, chopped
2 tablespoons minced parsley
1 cup bread crumbs
1 egg
Mayonnaise
Parmesan cheese, freshly grated

Chop mushroom stems and sauté in butter. Add onions and parsley and sauté. Add bread crumb mix and egg and stir lightly. Stuff mushroom caps, topping each with ½ teaspoon mayonnaise. Sprinkle with Parmesan cheese and place under broiler to brown lightly.

Duchess Potatoes

2 pounds potatoes, peeled
2 tablespoons butter
Salt, pepper and nutmeg to taste
2 whole eggs
2 egg yolks

Cut potatoes in pieces and boil in salted water until soft but not mushy. Drain and dry them out by shaking the pan over the fire. Mash well with butter and seasonings. Beat eggs together and beat into yolks. When ready to serve, force through a pastry tube to make rosettes; brown under the broiler.

Artichoke Bottoms

1 can artichoke bottoms
1 garlic pod, minced
1 tablespoon olive oil
2 cans puréed green peas
1 teaspoon mint
Salt and pepper to taste
Pinch of sugar

Sauté garlic in olive oil until soft. Add artichoke bottoms and sauté until heated through. Season peas and heat in saucepan. Serve hot with peas piled on artichoke bottoms.

Other vegetables, such as cauliflower, baby carrots or turnips may be steamed until just done, seasoned with butter, salt and pepper with an herb or two to taste. *Spinach Soufflé* is another possibility.

Hearts of Romaine Salad
Serves 4

1 head Romaine lettuce

Thoroughly wash and rinse a head of Romaine lettuce. Dry and chill. Cut into quarters lengthwise. Place each quarter on an ice cold salad plate and serve with *Sour Cream Dressing* and croutons.

Sour Cream Dressing

8 ounces sour cream
¾ cup mayonnaise
3 tablespoons freshly grated
   Parmesan cheese
1 teaspoon garlic salt
1½ tablespoons buttermilk
1½ tablespoons sweet milk
1½ teaspoons coarsely cracked
   black pepper

Mix well and chill. May use more milk to thin dressing.

Croutons

Sliced white or whole wheat bread
Butter
Garlic salt
Herbs
Parmesan cheese
Paprika

Brush bread with melted butter. Cut into ½-inch cubes. Fry slowly in a skillet with a small amount of butter to which garlic salt and herbs have been added. Croutons can be sprinkled with Parmesan cheese and/or paprika. Croutons will keep in tin box several days.

Crème Caramel
Serves 6 to 8

2 cups sugar
6 eggs
1 cup sugar
½ teaspoon vanilla
½ teaspoon salt
6 cups milk, scalded

Melt sugar in heavy skillet and pour about 1 tablespoon in each custard cup. Beat eggs slightly, add sugar, vanilla and salt and slowly pour the scalded milk into eggs. Strain and pour into custard cups with caramelized sugar in bottom. Set in a pan of water. Bake at 300° until firm, about 40 minutes. Do not overcook. Refrigerate and serve unmolded on a plate.

1 teaspoon grated orange rind and 1 tablespoon orange juice can be substituted for the vanilla.

This recipe came from Bodine's, a very old restaurant in Madrid, Spain, where they call it a flan.

A LUNCHEON MENU IN THE GATE ROOM

May Wine
Hot Chicken Loaf
Baby New Potatoes and Peas
Spiced Peach Salad Mold
Chocolate Mousse

May Wine

½ cup dried woodruff
¼ cup superfine granulated sugar
½ cup cognac
2 bottles Moselle or Rhine wine
1 bottle champagne
½ cup whole fresh strawberries

Tie woodruff in a square of cheesecloth. Mix sugar, cognac, ½ bottle wine and woodruff in a pitcher. Cover and let stand overnight. Strain into punch bowl containing ice cubes. Add remaining wine and champagne. Float strawberries on top. Serve in stemmed glasses.

May Wine is a refreshing drink for a party during the delightful month for which it is named.

Hot Chicken Loaf
Serves 12

1 large hen
2 celery stalks
2 bay leaves
6 whole peppercorns
1 teaspoon salt
2 tablespoons butter
2 tablespoons flour
1 cup milk
1 teaspoon parsley, chopped
1 cup rice, cooked
1 teaspoon pepper
1 teaspoon paprika
1 cup red pepper, chopped
1 cup onions, chopped

Cut 1 cup meat from the hen boiled with the onion, celery stalks, bay leaves, whole peppercorn and salt. Brown 2 tablespoons flour in 2 tablespoons melted butter. Pour over the chicken, adding the parsley and cooked rice, red pepper, celery, onion, garlic, boiled eggs and chicken stock. Pour into a buttered rectangular pan. Sprinkle the top with buttered cracker crumbs and chopped pecans. Bake at 350° 45 minutes or until firm.

1 cup celery, chopped
1 clove garlic, finely chopped
6 hard-boiled eggs, finely chopped
1 cup chicken stock
1 cup buttered cracker crumbs
1 cup pecans

MUSHROOM SAUCE:
2 tablespoons butter
1 cup fresh mushrooms, sliced
2 tablespoons flour
1 onion, finely chopped
Salt and pepper to taste
¼ teaspoon boveril
2 cups thin cream

Melt butter and sauté mushrooms. Brown flour in same pan. Add onion, salt, pepper, boveril and cream, stirring, to make a thin sauce. Serve over *Chicken Loaf* which has been cut in squares.

Hot Chicken Loaf is a good luncheon dish for a large crowd. Mother Witt used to serve this at the Sigma Chi house in Fayetteville.

Baby New Potatoes and Peas
Serves 8

1 pound fresh green peas, shelled
1 pound new potatoes
Pinch sugar
Salt and pepper to taste
1 tablespoon mint leaves, chopped
1 tablespoon parsley, chopped

Steam new peas in small amount of water, a pinch of sugar and covered with a lettuce leaf just a few minutes. Drain and add a pinch of sugar, salt, pepper, crushed mint leaves and a pat of butter. Peel potatoes around the middle, leaving part of the skin. Steam potatoes until just tender. Drain and season with butter, salt, pepper, chopped parsley and mint mixed together.

Spiced Peach Salad Mold
Serves 10 to 12

½ cup cold water
3 tablespoons gelatin
1 #3 can pickled peaches
2 tablespoons lemon juice
1 cup orange juice
Water

Soften gelatin in cold water and dissolve by setting container in pan of hot water. Drain peaches, reserving juice. Halve peaches and remove seeds. Add enough water to peach juice, lemon juice and orange juice to make 6 cups altogether and add dissolved gelatin mixture. Place peach halves in 6-quart mold and carefully pour juices into mold. Refrigerate until solid. Unmold and serve with meats or with a buffet dinner.

Chocolate Mousse
Serves 8

1 package semi-sweet chocolate
1 cup granulated sugar
1 teaspoon powdered coffee
½ cup water
10 egg yolks
2 teaspoons vanilla
10 egg whites
½ pint heavy cream, whipped
½ cup slivered almonds, toasted

Melt together in top of double boiler chocolate, sugar, coffee and water. Stir until very smooth. Remove pan from heat to a pan of cold water. Stir until cool. Add well beaten egg yolks and vanilla. The mixture should be semi-fluid. Beat egg whites until stiff and fold in chocolate mixture gently but thoroughly. Pour into individual cups and chill 6 to 8 hours. Serve with sweetened whipped cream and toasted almonds.

Chocolate Mousse is always a bit of heaven—and is easy to make and to serve.

RUSSIAN BUFFET TABLE

Buckwheat Blini
Kulebiaka
Molded Beet Salad
Cucumber Mousse
Yogurt or Sour Cream Dressing
Chicken Liver Pate
Charlotte Russe

The Russian Buffet Table, or "zakuska," evolved as an array of "small bites" to give guests at country houses who might have come from a long distance in sub-zero weather sustenance and keep them in good spirits while waiting for dinner. This is an adaptation of the "zakuska" that will keep you in good spirits—and also suffice for dinner.

Buckwheat Blini
Makes about 36 blini

"Blini" have a distinctive taste quite unlike the average griddlecake, mainly because they are made with a yeast batter. Their preparation should start about 6 hours before you plan to serve them. When the batter is complete, the pancakes must be cooked and served at once.

½ cup lukewarm water
1 ½ tablespoons active dry yeast
1 cup buckwheat flour
1 ½ cups white flour
2 cups lukewarm milk
3 egg yolks, lightly beaten
½ teaspoon salt
1 teaspoon sugar
½ pound butter, melted and cooled
2 cups sour cream
3 egg whites

Pour the lukewarm water into a small bowl and sprinkle the yeast over it. Let stand until softened and stir to dissolve. Set in a warm, draft–free spot 3 to 5 minutes, or until the mixture almost doubles in volume.

In a large mixing bowl, combine ½ cup buckwheat flour and the white flour. Make a deep well in center and pour in 1 cup of the milk and the yeast mixture. Stir the flour into the liquid ingredients with a large wooden spoon, then beat vigorously until the mixture is smooth. Cover the bowl loosely with a towel and set aside in a warm spot 3 hours, or until it doubles in volume.

Stir the batter thoroughly and beat in remaining ½ cup buckwheat flour. Cover with a towel and let the batter rest in the warm spot another 2 hours. Again stir the batter and gradually beat in the remaining cup of lukewarm milk and the egg yolks, salt, sugar, 3 tablespoons of the melted butter and 3 tablespoons of the sour cream.

Beat the egg whites in a large bowl until they form stiff peaks on the beater when it is lifted from the bowl. With a rubber spatula, fold the egg whites gently into the batter, cover loosely with a towel and let the batter rest in the warm spot 30 minutes.

Preheat oven to 200°. Lightly brush the bottom of a heavy skillet with melted butter. Set the pan over high heat until a drop of water flicked across its surface evaporates instantly. Pour in about 3 tablespoons of the batter for each pancake and fry 2 or 3 minutes. Turn the pancake over and cook another 2 minutes or until golden brown.

Transfer the pancakes to an ovenproof dish and keep them warm in the oven while you cook the remaining pancakes, adding butter to the pan as needed.

Serve the blini hot, accompanied by bowls of melted butter and sour cream, smoked salmon and red or black caviar.

Buckwheat Blini are wonderful to serve with cocktails before any meal. They originated as a celebration of the winter solstice in ancient Russia. The little round pancakes recalled the sun's golden image and were eaten in an effort to keep warm.

Kulebiaka
(Russian Salmon in Pastry)
Serves 10 to 12

Kulebiaka is the Russian version of Beef Wellington. It makes a beautiful presentation, brought to the table and sliced, and can be served hot or at room temperature. The recipe may seem complicated, but it is well worth the effort! Substituting canned salmon (red sockeye) for the fresh is a time-saver. The Kulebiaka may be made in advance and frozen before baking.

Variations of the salmon filling can be chicken, meat or cabbage, making it very versatile.

PASTRY:
4 cups flour, all–purpose
1 teaspoon salt
½ pound unsalted butter, chilled
7 tablespoons vegetable shortening
10 to 12 tablespoons ice water

Combine in a large chilled bowl the flour, salt, butter and shortening. Work butter and shortening into flour using a pastry blender or your fingertips until they blend and resemble coarse meal. Pour 10 tablespoons of the water over the mixture all at once. Toss together lightly and gather into a ball. If the dough seems crumbly, add up to 2 tablespoons more ice water by drops. Divide the dough in half, dust each half with flour and wrap them separately in plastic wrap. Refrigerate 3 hours, or until firm.

SALMON FILLING:
2 cups dry white wine
1 cup onions, coarsely chopped
½ cup celery, coarsely chopped
1 cup carrots, scraped and coarsely chopped
10 whole black peppercorns
Salt to taste
2½ pounds fresh salmon in 1 piece (or substitute 2½ pounds canned red salmon)
8 tablespoons butter, unsalted
3 hard-boiled eggs, finely chopped
½ pound fresh mushrooms, thinly sliced
3 tablespoons fresh lemon juice
Freshly ground black pepper
3 cups onion, finely chopped
½ cup unconverted, long grain white rice
1 cup chicken stock, fresh or canned
2 tablespoons parsley, minced

If using fresh salmon, combine 3 quarts water, wine, onion, carrots, peppercorns and salt in a 4- to 6-quart pan. Bring to a boil over high heat and lower the salmon into the liquid and reduce heat to low. Simmer 10 minutes or until fish flakes easily with a fork. Drain. Transfer salmon to a large bowl, remove the skin and bones and separate into small flakes. (If using canned salmon, omit the first 7 ingredients, drain, check for bones and flake.)

Melt 4 tablespoons of the butter in a heavy skillet set over high heat. Add mushrooms and all but 1 tablespoon of the onions, reduce the heat and cook 3 to 5 minutes until soft. With a slotted spoon transfer onions and mushrooms to a small bowl and toss them with lemon juice, salt and a few grindings of pepper. Now melt the other 4 tablespoons butter in the skillet and sauté the remaining onion until soft. Stir in the rice and cook 2 or 3 minutes, stirring constantly, until each grain is coated with butter. Pour in the chicken stock, bring to a boil and cover the pan tightly. Reduce heat to low and simmer 12 minutes, or until liquid is absorbed and rice is fluffy. Turn off the heat, stir in the parsley and dill. Add the mushrooms and onions, rice and chopped eggs to the bowl of salmon and toss lightly. Taste for seasoning. Refrigerate until ready to assemble.

⅓ cup fresh dill, minced or ¾
    teaspoon dried dill
½ cup mayonnaise

ASSEMBLY:
2 tablespoons butter
2 egg yolks
½ cup cream
1 tablespoon melted butter
1 cup sour cream
Dill

Preheat oven to 400°. Place 1 ball of dough on a lightly floured surface and roll it into a rough rectangle about 1 inch thick. Dust with flour and roll until the dough is about ⅛ inch thick, trim it to a rectangle 7×16 inches. Coat a large cookie sheet with 2 tablespoons butter, drape the pastry over the rolling pin and unroll it over the cookie sheet. Place the filling along the length of the pastry, leaving a 1-inch border of dough exposed around it. With a pastry brush, brush the exposed rim of dough with the egg yolk and cream mixture. Roll the other ball of dough into a rectangle about 9×18 inches, drape over the pin and unroll over the filling. Seal the edges by pressing down hard with the back of a fork, or use your finger tips or a pastry crimper to pinch the edges into narrow pleats. Cut out a 1-inch circle from the center of the top of the dough to allow steam to escape while baking. Gather any remaining pastry scraps and roll them out again for decorating the top. With a pastry cutter or sharp knife cut out leaf shapes (or diamonds or other desired shapes). Coat the entire surface of the dough with the egg and cream mixture, apply the pastry shapes and refrigerate 20 minutes. Pour 1 tablespoon of melted butter in the hole and bake in the center of the oven 1 hour, or until golden brown. Serve at once, accompanied by a bowl of sour cream and dill.

Molded Beet Salad
Serves 4 to 6

3 cups beets, cooked and chopped
1 package lemon jello
¾ cup celery, chopped
2 tablespoons onion, finely
    chopped
2 tablespoons horseradish
½ teaspoon salt
3 tablespoons vinegar
1 teaspoon capers
2 tablespoons sour cream or
    mayonnaise

Drain beets and reserve juice. Purée beets in food processor. Add enough water to beet juice to make 1½ cups. Dissolve jello in liquid and stir in vegetables. Pour into 1-quart mold and chill until firm. Garnish with dollop of sour cream or mayonnaise mixed with capers.

Cucumber Mousse
Serves 6

1 package lime jello
1 cup boiling water
1 8-ounce package cream cheese
1 cup cold water
⅔ cup mayonnaise
⅔ cup sour cream
⅓ cup coffee cream
1½ stalks celery, diced
1 cucumber, peeled and diced

YOGURT OR SOUR CREAM DRESSING:
⅔ cup yogurt or sour cream
2 tablespoons cider vinegar
Salt and pepper to taste

Dissolve jello and cheese in boiling water, add cold water and cool. Add remaining ingredients and fold gently until well mixed. Pour into 1-quart mold which has been rinsed in cold water and chill overnight. Garnish with thin slices of cucumber and serve with *Yogurt or Sour Cream Dressing.*

Chicken Liver Pâté

¾ pound chicken livers
Salt and freshly ground pepper to taste
¼ bay leaf, broken in small pieces
⅛ teaspoon thyme
⅛ teaspoon allspice
⅛ teaspoon cinnamon
Pinch of cayenne pepper
¼ pound butter or melted chicken fat
½ cup thinly sliced shallots
¼ pound mushrooms, thinly sliced
1 tablespoon cognac
Chopped raw onions (optional)

Pick over the livers and cut away and discard any tough connective tissues. Place in a bowl and add salt, pepper, bay leaf, thyme, allspice, cinnamon and cayenne. Heat the butter in a heavy skillet and add the shallots and mushroooms. Cook, stirring often, until the mushrooms give up their liquid. Cook until most of this liquid evaporates. Add the livers and seasonings and stir. Cook, stirring occasionally, about 10 minutes. Pour and scrape this mixture into the container of a food processor or blender. Add the cognac and blend to a fine purée. Spoon and scrape the mousse into a small serving dish. Smooth over the top. Let cool. Chill. Serve with thinly sliced rye bread and chopped onion.

Charlotte Russe
Serves 6

12 ladyfingers, split in half
   lengthwise
4 egg yolks
½ cup sugar
1 cup milk
1-inch piece of vanilla bean
2 tablespoons plain gelatin
¼ cup cold water
1 tablespoon brandy
½ cup sour cream
½ pint whipping cream
12 almond macaroons
Optional: ½ cup slivered almonds,
   toasted

Arrange the ladyfingers in the bottom of a 1-quart soufflé dish or charlotte mold, curved sides down. Arrange remaining ladyfingers standing up around the sides of the mold, overlapping slightly.

Beat egg yolks in the top of a double boiler or metal bowl. Gradually add sugar, beating constantly until thick and lemon colored. In a small pan, heat the milk and vanilla bean until bubbles appear around the edge. Remove the bean, and slowly stir the hot milk into the eggs, beating constantly. Cook over low heat, stirring, until mixture thickens into a custard and coats the spoon. Remove from heat immediately.

Soften gelatin in cold water and stir it into the custard. Set the bowl of custard over a bowl of ice and stir until cool and thick. Stir in the brandy. Whip together the sour cream and whipping cream until stiff. Gently fold it into the custard. Crumble macaroons and fold into mixture. Pour the mixture into the mold, smooth the top and cover with plastic wrap. Refrigerate 4 to 5 hours. Unmold by inverting a serving plate on top and then turning them both upside down. Or serve the charlotte in the mold with toasted almonds sprinkled over the top.

The addition of the macaroons gives this version of *Charlotte Russe* a crunchy, almond flavor. Raspberry preserves spread over the top are delicious.

Holidays on the Island

Easter, Mother's Day and Thanksgiving dinners are especially popular at the Red Apple. Many people make a family tradition of driving to Eden Isle and having dinner with their families without the effort involved in cooking. They know the traditional meal will be served in an elegant but festive atmosphere, and they will enjoy greeting old friends. I have adapted our family traditional meals for these occasions for the large crowds served at the Red Apple.

Holidays are a time of gatherings, so it is usually a big meal in terms of the numbers of dishes. It is also the time for family traditions to be born and recalled year after year. All of us have listened to our children recalling special meals on holidays like Christmas or Thanksgiving. Sometimes we don't recognize their larger-than-life memories.

The Inn serves an elaborate buffet on Easter for over 300 people, which the kitchen starts preparing before five o'clock in the morning. I have chosen a few of the dishes here that you might want to select from in planning a family Easter dinner that won't exhaust the cook.

EASTER DINNER

Spring Lamb
Turnip and Onion Casserole
Perfection Mold
Fresh Fruit Salad
Hot Rolls
Parsley Buttered New Potatoes
Broccoli Soufflé
Strawberry Shortcake

Spring Lamb

1 leg of lamb
3 to 4 cloves of garlic
Salt and pepper
Your favorite mixture of herbs
¼ cup Dijon mustard
¼ cup horseradish
½ cup red wine vinegar
3 bay leaves

Remove the excess fat. Make slits in fat and insert slivers of garlic cloves. Season with herbs. Coat well with prepared mustard and horseradish (equal parts). Put ½ cup of red–cider vinegar in the bottom of the pan. Place 3 bay leaves in the pan and bake slowly, or lamb will dry out. Bake at 325°.

Turnip and Onion Casserole
Serves 8 to 10

2 ½ pounds yellow turnips or
   rutabagas (about 8 cups diced)
3 tablespoons butter
⅔ cup onions, finely diced
1 tablespoon flour
¾ cup beef bouillon
¼ teaspoon sage
Salt and pepper
2 to 3 tablespoons fresh minced
   parsley
½ cup heavy cream

Peel the turnips, cut into ½-inch cubes. Drop into boiling salted water and boil uncovered 3 to 5 minutes, or until slightly tender. Drain.

Add the butter to the pan. Stir in the onions, cover and cook slowly 5 minutes without browning. Blend in the flour and cook slowly about 2 minutes. Remove from heat, beat in the bouillon, return to heat and bring to a simmer. Add the sage, then fold in the turnips. Season to taste with salt and pepper.

Cover the pan and simmer slowly 20 to 30 minutes, or until turnips are tender. If sauce is too liquid, uncover and boil slowly several minutes until reduced and thickened. Adjust seasoning. Add ½ cup heated (not boiled) heavy cream. (May be cooked ahead. Cool uncovered; cover and simmer a few moments before serving.) To serve, fold in the parsley and turn into a hot serving dish.

Perfection Mold
Serves 8

2 tablespoons unflavored gelatin
½ cup cold water
1 cup boiling water
1 teaspoon salt
¼ cup tarragon vinegar
¼ cup cider vinegar
⅓ cup sugar
2½ cups grated cabbage
1 stalk celery, chopped
2 sweet red peppers, chopped
1 green pepper, chopped
1 cup pecans, chopped
2 3-ounce packages cream cheese, softened
1 3-ounce package blue cheese, softened
Cream

Soften gelatin in cold water. Dissolve in boiling water. Add salt, vinegars and sugar. Allow this mixture to cool. Then add cabbage, celery, red pepper, green pepper and pecans. Pour into oiled mold and chill until firm. Serve with cream cheese and blue cheese which have been blended together with enough cream to soften.

Strawberry Shortcake
Serves 6

1 recipe *Pastry*
1 quart strawberries
¼ to ½ cup sugar
Kirsch or brandy

Roll out chilled pastry dough to a thickness of about ¼ inch. With biscuit cutter, cut into rounds and bake at 400° until lightly browned. Clean and slice strawberries and sweeten to taste. (A little Kirsch or brandy may be added to strawberries at this point—optional!). On dessert plate place 1 round of pastry topped by strawberries. Add another pastry round and strawberries and another layer. Top last round of strawberries with sweetened whipped cream. Rest a pretty strawberry on top and serve.

Thanksgiving

Thanksgiving is always a very special celebration at the Red Apple Inn. Everyone puts forth their best efforts in gratitude for the multitude of blessings received during the year. I remember Elna turning out her luscious pecan and pumpkin pies and hot rolls and Pauline mixing up the delicious turkey dressing and vegetables—sweet potatoes and rutabagas—and all kinds of salads.

My job on Thanksgiving Day is to season the dressing for the expected crowd of over 400 people. One Thanksgiving Herbert Thomas appeared early at the Inn to inspect the proceedings. He tasted the Turkey Dressing and decided it needed a dose of sage and proceeded to season it. Awhile later I arrived—not knowing he had been there—and added the sage before I tasted it. Needless to say, the dressing did not get raves that year but no one had the heart to mention it. Sage is not an herb to overdo!

Preparations for the extensive Thanksgiving buffet start at 4:00 A.M. with over 400 people expected. I have chosen the dishes here that are my family's favorites for a dinner at home. Each person brings his or her specialty to make it easy on the hosts.

THANKSGIVING DINNER

Iced Danish Mary
Cheese Straws
Turkey and Giblet Gravy
Eden Isle Corn Bread Dressing
Scalloped Oysters
Sweet Potatoes in Orange Cups
Brussel Sprouts in Consommé
Grapefruit and Avocado Salad
Cranberry Sauce
Hot Rolls with Butter
Ambrosia
Elna's Pumpkin Pie

Iced Danish Mary
Serves 6

3 cups tomato juice
¼ cup fresh lemon juice
Salt to taste
1 teaspoon Worcestershire sauce
Tabasco sauce to taste
9 ounces aquavit or vodka
2 egg whites
Dill weed

Blend ingredients except dill in a blender or food processor. Freeze in one of the new iceless freezers and serve topped with dill weed for garnish. Or freeze in a container in the freezer, remove and blend in the blender or food processor again and refreeze.

This is a drink designed to keep the cooks cool as the kitchen heats up with roasting turkey and all the trimmings.

Cheese Straws

½ cup butter
1 cup flour
1 cup grated sharp cheddar
⅛ teaspoon salt
Dash cayenne pepper

Mix butter and cheese. Season with salt and cayenne. Work in flour. Roll thin and cut into strips or put through a cookie gun in strips. Bake at 325° until lightly browned. They burn quickly.

Turkey and Giblet Gravy
Serves about 20

1 16–to 18-pound turkey
1 cup onions, chopped
1 cup celery, chopped
1 cup carrots, chopped
Salt and pepper
¼ cup butter
¼ cup olive oil

We preferred to purchase a fresh turkey instead of frozen, and liked to have the younger ones (about 16 to 18 pounds) as they tend to be more tender, and require less cooking time.

Thoroughly clean turkey inside and out, and pat dry with a towel. Place onion, celery and carrots into each cavity. Rub salt and pepper over the outside of each turkey. Then rub with a good portion of butter mixed with olive oil. Place in a large roasting pan with sides about 4 inches high and cover loosely with foil. Bake at 325° as long as it takes at 16 minutes per pound. That amounts to about 4 hours for a 16-pound bird. The turkey should be basted about 4 times during its cooking period with juices that have

accumulated in the roasting pan. The aluminum foil should be removed during the last 30 minutes to allow for browning. The turkey is done when the leg moves easily when twisted. Cooking too long will dry the meat. A turkey will bring much eating pleasure, if it is well prepared.

While the turkey is cooking, place the clean giblets and the neck in a saucepan with 3 cups of water (or to cover), onion, celery, carrot and bay leaf. Simmer this until all the meat is tender. A dash of chicken broth granules or 2 chicken broth cubes can be added, along with pepper. Remove the meat with a slotted spoon, and thicken the liquid with the flour. Chop the giblets and add to the gravy. Add 2 hard-boiled eggs to give it color. Juices from the roasting pan may be added to this.

GRAVY:

1 onion, chopped
2 ribs celery, chopped
1 carrot, chopped
1 bay leaf
2 chicken broth cubes
¼ cup flour
Pepper to taste
2 hard-boiled eggs

Eden Isle Corn Bread Dressing
Serves 10

3 tablespoons butter
1 cup onion, chopped
1 cup celery, chopped
1 pan *Skillet Corn Bread,* broken
  into crumbs
A few stale biscuits, crumbled
½ teaspoon salt (to taste)
¾ teaspoon pepper
¼ teaspoon nutmeg
¼ teaspoon thyme
1 tablespoon sugar
2 cups boiling beef bouillon (more if
  needed to moisten bread)
Optional, one or more of the
  following:
  1 cup sautéed, chopped oyster
  1 cup chopped fresh mushroom
  1 cup chopped pecans
  1 can chopped Chinese water
    chestnuts

Sauté onion and celery in butter. In large bowl or pan, mix onion and celery with corn bread, biscuits, spices and one or more optional ingredients. Pour boiling bouillon over mixture until moist. Mix well. Put into buttered casserole and bake at 400° until brown on top—about 30 minutes.

Hint: do not chop oysters, mushrooms or nuts too finely.

Scalloped Oysters
Serves 4 to 6

2 cups oysters, freshly shucked and
    their liquid
½ cup cracker crumbs
½ cup bread crumbs
½ stick butter
¼ cup sherry
½ pint cream
Salt and pepper to taste
Pinch cayenne pepper

Mix together cracker crumbs, bread crumbs and melted butter. Put a thin layer of this mixture in the bottom of a well buttered baking dish and cover it with a cup of the oysters and some liquor. Sprinkle the oysters with salt, pepper and cayenne. Add another layer of the crumb mixture and the remaining oysters and repeat the seasoning. Add the cream and finish with the rest of the crumbs, sprinkle with sherry and dot thickly with bits of butter. Set the dish in a hot oven (375°) 15 minutes.

Sweet Potatoes in Orange Cups
Serves 12

6 large sweet potatoes
Salt and pepper to taste
4 tablespoons butter
½ cup orange juice
¼ cup brown sugar, sifted
¼ teaspoon nutmeg
½ cup chopped pecans, optional
12 orange halves, serrated
12 marshmallows

Boil sweet potatoes in water until tender. Cool and peel. Purée sweet potatoes in food processor or mixer. Add butter and blend. Add orange juice, sugar, nutmeg and blend. With a sharp knife, cut the edges of the orange halves in a serrated pattern. Fill with the sweet potato mixture. Just before serving, heat in medium oven, top with marshmallows and heat again until marshmallow is melted.

Brussel Sprouts in Consommé
Serves 6 to 8

1 pound fresh brussel sprouts
2 cans beef consommé
Pepper to taste
Freshly grated Parmesan cheese

Trim fresh sprouts and cut an "X" on the bottom of each so they will cook evenly. Boil in consommé about 15 minutes or until tender, but still a bright green color. Add pepper, sprinkle with Parmesan cheese and serve.

Grapefruit and Avocado Salad
Serves 10

4 grapefruits
4 avocados
1 red onion

Peel grapefruit and cut into sections. Peel avocado and cut into sections. Peel red onion and slice thinly. Combine with *Vinaigrette Dressing* and serve on lettuce cups.

Elna's Pumpkin Pie
Serves 8

2 cups canned pumpkin
1 cup granulated sugar
½ cup brown sugar
¼ teaspoon salt
2 eggs
2 teaspoons cinnamon
1 teaspoon nutmeg
Dash cloves
1 cup evaporated milk

Beat eggs slightly. Add sugar, pumpkin and spices in succession. Add milk and bake in prebaked pie shell at 350° about 30 to 35 minutes or until firm in center.

This recipe is from Elna Bolen, who was the very talented dessert cook at the Red Apple Inn for many years.

Christmas

The only day of the year the Red Apple Inn is closed is Christmas Day, so that all the employees can spend the day with their families. In our family breakfast, after the early morning package opening, was a major event looked forward to even more than the late afternoon Christmas dinner. The grandchildren always make sure they are around for this meal—even the vegetarians in the crowd relish the once-a-year opportunity to eat quail.

Herbert was an avid quail hunter, and we had no shortage of wild quail. The entire area surrounding Eden Isle has been a paradise for hunters. However in recent years the wild quail are becoming scarce. If you're lucky, you may know a hunter who will share his bounty. Or you might try some of the farm-raised quail that have become popular in restaurants, and now in supermarkets. They are a little tenderer, although not quite as flavorful, as the wild quail. Some of them have been deboned and are easy to cook. All are a source of low fat protein.

CHRISTMAS BREAKFAST

Orange Juice with Champagne
Christmas Quail and Gravy
Fried Sweet Potatoes
Sourdough Biscuits
Tiny Sausages
Soft Scrambled Eggs

Orange Juice with Champagne

I would like to say that we serve freshly squeezed orange juice on Christmas morning, but I'm afraid no one would believe we are that organized. When Santa is ringing the sleigh bells to wake up the household, we are lucky to have someone in the kitchen who will thaw the frozen juice for the morning eye opener. A few spirited family members will start the day with an Orange Blossom, which is just a mixture of orange juice and champagne—and each person will determine his or her own proportions.

Christmas Quail and Gravy

Wild or domesticated large quail (at least 1 per person)
Milk
All–purpose flour
Salt and pepper
Vegetable oil
Garlic
Beef bouillon cubes
Bacon
Worcestershire sauce, BV sauce, or Kitchen Bouquet

Marinate quail overnight in milk. When ready to cook, remove and pat dry with a towel. Rub each quail with a cut clove of garlic. Drip each one with Worcestershire sauce, BV sauce or Kitchen Bouquet. Wrap each quail in ½ slice of bacon secured with toothpicks. Place in paper sack with flour, salt and pepper and shake well. Heat vegetable oil ¼ inch in cast iron skillet at ¾ heat. When skillet is hot, place quail in skillet and cook until brown on all sides. Then turn heat down, add water to fill ⅔ of skillet. Add 2 bouillon cubes and Worcestershire sauce, BV or Kitchen Bouquet. Let simmer about 30 minutes. Skim off the oil from the top of the gravy with a spoon. Serve on toast with the gravy accompanied by brown rice or grits and soft scrambled eggs.

This recipe for quail has been passed down for generations in the Thomas family. It traveled from the Carolinas to Georgia and then to Arkansas. Christmas morning is always celebrated with a quail breakfast.

Fried Sweet Potatoes

Sweet potatoes
Vegetable oil to fry
Powdered sugar

Peel and slice sweet potatoes into ¼-inch slices. Parboil 5 minutes. Drain and pat dry with paper towel. Fry in hot vegetable oil until brown on one side and turn. Drain on paper towels, sprinkle with powdered sugar and serve.

Sourdough Biscuits

Make *Buttermilk Biscuits* the night before. Roll out and let sit in warm place overnight. Bake when ready for breakfast.

CHRISTMAS GOODIES

Orange Pecans

2 cups sugar
¾ cup water
1 teaspoon vinegar
¼ teaspoon cream of tartar
Grated rind of 1 orange
3 tablespoons orange juice
3 cups pecan halves

Boil sugar, water, vinegar and cream of tartar together until softball stage. Add grated rind of orange and orange juice. Beat until creamy. Add pecans, stir until well covered, then spread on waxed paper. When cool, separate into pieces.

Sour Cream Fudge

2 squares bitter chocolate
2 cups sugar
⅔ cup sour cream
1 teaspoon vanilla
Small pinch salt
10 squares semi-sweet chocolate,
  melted
2 cups pecans, chopped

Melt bitter chocolate in top of double boiler. Add sugar and blend well. Stir in sour cream and remove to direct heat. Stir well until dissolved, scraping sugar from sides of pan. Cover with lid and bring very slowly to a soft boil. Remove from fire. Pour onto porcelain or metal platter and cool. Add vanilla and salt and beat until creamy and stiff. (It will turn a lighter brown). Form into small balls. Roll in semi-sweet chocolate and then chopped pecans. Will keep several weeks in tightly covered container—unless someone has discovered them!

The tricky part of this recipe is to keep it from turning to sugar. Scraping the sides of the pan and covering with a lid both help. If it does get sugary, you may recook it.

Sour Cream Fudge is the treasured recipe of the South Louisiana family of a dear friend, and my family has adopted it as an essential part of Christmas. The season hasn't really begun until we have each made at least one batch of this chocolate delight for gift-giving and for drop–in guests.

Lemon Christmas Cake

1 pound butter
2 cups sugar
6 eggs, beaten slightly
3 cups cake flour, sifted
¼ teaspoon salt
1 teaspoon baking powder
1 box white raisins
1 pound pecans, chopped
¼ cup flour
2 ounces lemon extract

Cream butter and sugar in mixer or bowl of food processer. Add eggs and mix. Sift together flour, salt and baking powder and mix with butter, sugar and egg mixture. Dredge raisins and nut meats in flour and add to mixture. Add lemon extract and mix.

Bake in 2 well greased loaf pans in 325° oven 1 hour. Leave in oven 1 more hour with oven turned off. Remove from pans and cool completely. Wrap well and store in refrigerator or freezer. (I pour rum or bourbon over it before wrapping in foil.)

This recipe originated in Memphis, and makes a wonderful cake to give at Christmas. It is not as rich as traditional fruit cake. It is wonderful toasted for breakfast!

Wassail
Makes 12 cups

2 cups cranberry juice
6 cups apple cider
1 teaspoon bitters
¼ cup sugar
1 stick cinnamon
1 teaspoon allspice
1 orange studded with cloves
4 cups rum

The orange may be studded with the cloves the day before. Heat all ingredients except rum and keep hot during party. Pour about half into a punch bowl and add half the rum. Replenish as necessary. Mixture may be kept hot in a large coffee urn.

We like the tradition of *Wassail* at Christmas. This recipe for a large crowd is good because it is not too sweet. And it gives the house a wonderful aroma.

Independence Day

Picnics and fireworks have both been outstanding features of Eden Isle's 4th of July celebrations. For years we had an island picnic (which always included Dr. Jim Shelton's famous basting sauce) until the fireworks display became the central feature of the holiday. Now visitors pour into the area at a growth rate of about 10,000 per year to watch the fantastic display from land and water. Fired by Pyro-Spectacular of Rialto, California, the company chosen to produce the fireworks for the Statue of Liberty celebration, the display is a spectacular thank you gift to Cleburne County from "The Smell of Christmas" Company, Aromatique, that got its start on Eden Isle. Residents on the hills overlooking the lake say the lights on the thousands of boats add even more drama to the fireworks in the sky. It has become a perfect night to invite family and a few friends for a picnic on board the boat to watch the sunset and the moon as it rises over Sugar Loaf Mountain, enjoy the food and be a part of the festivities on the lake.

Our family favorites include casual yet festive fare such as the traditional Southern fried chicken and potato salad, tomato sandwiches, fresh fruits and perhaps hand--turned ice cream and brownies for dessert. For more elegant outings we like to add chilled champagne served in crystal glasses and a bright tablecloth and jazz up the menu a little bit. For the 4th of July we might choose either of these menus:

PICNIC FARE

Shrimp and Cheese Ball
Tomato Sandwiches
Cucumber Salad
Thinly Sliced Cold Roast Beef
Rye Bread with Raspberry Mustard
Bowl of Fresh Strawberries
Caramel Brownies

Shrimp and Cheese Ball

2 8-ounce packages cream cheese
4 ounces sharp cheese, grated
2 tablespoons Worcestershire
   sauce
1 teaspoon garlic salt
1 tablespoon Durkee's dressing
1 tablespoon lemon juice
5 ounces shrimp, peeled, cooked
   and chopped

Let ingredients come to room temperature and mix. Add cream if necessary to blend well. Form into a ball and chill overnight. Decorate with minced parsley and paprika. Serve with crackers.

Tomato Sandwiches

Fresh tomatoes, peeled and sliced
Whole wheat or white bread
Homemade Mayonnaise
Chopped basil
Freshly ground black pepper

Cut crusts off bread. Spread with mayonnaise and place several tomato slices on each sandwich. Season with basil and sprinkle with pepper.

Cucumber Salad
Serves 4

1 large cucumber
½ cup wine vinegar
1 tablespoon water
1 tablespoon sugar
¼ teaspoon salt
Dash white pepper
2 tablespoons parsley or dill,
   minced

Peel and thinly slice cucumber and place into a bowl or china serving dish. Sprinkle with wine vinegar, water, sugar, salt, pepper and parsley or dill. Chill in refrigerator 2 hours.

Cucumber Salad is also good with broiled trout.

Caramel Brownies

¼ cup butter or margarine
1 cup brown sugar
1 egg
1 teaspoon vanilla
½ cup flour
1 teaspoon baking powder
½ cup pecans, chopped

Melt butter with brown sugar and set aside to cool. Add eggs and mix. Sift flour with baking powder and add to mixture. Add pecans and stir. Pour into greased rectangular 8×8-inch pan and bake at 350° about 30 minutes. Cut into squares when cool.

MENU

Cornish Hens Baked in Wine
Fresh Pineapple and Strawberries
Cucumber Sandwiches with Dill
Deviled Eggs with Asparagus
Chocolate Fudge Cup Cakes

Cornish Hens Baked in Wine
Serves 6 to 12

6 Rock Cornish hens
6 garlic cloves
6 teaspoons dried tarragon
Salt and pepper
Garlic salt
¾ cup butter
¾ cup dry white wine
1 tablespoon tarragon
1 bunch watercress

In each hen place 1 clove of garlic, 1 teaspoon of dried tarragon, ¼ teaspoon of salt and ⅛ teaspoon pepper. Sprinkle outside liberally with garlic salt; chill.

Roast hens 45 minutes in large shallow pan at 450°, basting with sauce made from melted butter, white wine and 1 tablespoon tarragon. Arrange birds on bed of watercress on serving platter; pour drippings from roasting pan over hens. To serve at room temperature for a picnic, cool and cut in half.

Cucumber Sandwiches with Dill

Whole wheat bread
Homemade Mayonnnaise
1 cucumber, peeled and thinly
    sliced
Salt and pepper
Dill

Cut crusts from bread. Spread with mayonnaise and cover with cucumber slices. Season. Cover tightly with plastic wrap.

Deviled Eggs with Asparagus

12 hard-boiled eggs
4 tablespoons mayonnaise
2 tablespoons Durkee's dressing
Salt and cayenne pepper to taste
1 can asparagus, drained
Pinch tarragon

Cut eggs in two and remove yolks from eggs. Mash with mayonnaise, Durkee's, salt and pepper, asparagus and seasoning. Fill egg whites with mixture. Garnish with raw asparagus and cayenne pepper.

Chocolate Fudge Cupcakes

4 squares semi-sweet chocolate
½ pound butter or margarine
1 cup flour
1¾ cup sugar
4 eggs
2 teaspoons vanilla
2 cups chopped pecans

Melt chocolate and butter in double boiler. Mix flour and sugar in a bowl and add eggs, one at a time. Stir as little as possible. Add melted chocolate. Stir in vanilla and pecans. Bake 25 or 30 minutes at 325° in paper muffin cups. Frost with frosting for *Sour Cream Chocolate Cake*.

Other Favorite Recipes

APPETIZERS

Roquefort Wafers

1 cup flour
7 tablespoons Roquefort cheese
7 tablespoons butter
4 teaspoons heavy cream
Pinch salt
1 egg yolk
Cayenne to taste

Cut cheese and butter into flour with a pastry cutter. Add cream, salt, egg and cayenne and mix well. Let rest in refrigerator 20 minutes. Shape into a long roll. Cover with plastic wrap and refrigerate 20 minutes longer. Slice thinly and bake on cookie sheet in 400° oven 8 to 10 minutes or until lighly browned. Remove very carefully from the cookie sheet, as they are delicate. These are scrumptious "as is" or spread with the following mixture.

FILLING:
3 egg yolks
⅔ cup heavy cream
Salt and cayenne to taste
5 tablespoons Roquefort cheese
3 tablespoons butter
1 teaspoon Kirsch

Mix and heat eggs, cream, salt and pepper over low heat. Beat in Roquefort and butter and cook until thickened. Flavor with Kirsch. Cool and spread on wafers.

This is an excellent recipe for serving while a crowd is waiting for lunch or dinner.

Mushrooms Stuffed with Oysters

1 quart fresh oysters
1 pound fresh mushrooms
2 tablespoons butter
6 green onions, chopped
2 tablespoons minced parsley
Parmesan cheese bread crumb mix
1 egg
Mayonnaise

Chop oysters and mushroom stems and sauté in butter. Add onions and parsley and sauté. Add bread crumb mix and egg and stir lightly. Stuff mushroom caps, add a dollop of mayonnaise atop each and place under broiler to brown lightly.

Mushrooms Stuffed with Escargots

1 pound fresh mushrooms
½ pound butter
2 cloves garlic, minced
2 shallots, minced
3 sprigs parsley, minced
2 7-ounce cans escargots or snails

Brush mushrooms clean. Remove stems and set aside. Make butter balls by combining softened butter, chopped garlic, shallots and parsley and roll into balls about the size of marbles. Chill in refrigerator. Place 1 snail into mushroom and firmly place 1 ball of seasoned butter on top of each snail. Run under broiler until butter is well melted and snail is drenched in butter. Serve 3 or 4 on small plate with parsley.

Hot Cheese Balls

1 cup cheddar cheese, grated
6 drops Worcestershire sauce
½ cup bread crumbs
1 egg, well beaten
Dash cayenne pepper
½ teaspoon salt
Cracker crumbs

Mix all ingredients except cracker crumbs. Shape into balls the size of a walnut. Roll balls in cracker crumbs. Fry at 375° in deep fat, drain and serve immediately.

These may be made ahead of time, chilled and fried just before serving.

Smoked Salmon Mousse

½ pound smoked salmon, cut up
½ pound cream cheese, softened
⅓ cup scallions, chopped
¼ cup dill, finely chopped
Juice of half a lemon
Freshly ground pepper to taste
Asco sauce to taste
Chopped raw onion
Drained capers
Optional: 2 tablespoons aquavit

Combine all of the ingredients, except the chopped onion and capers, in food processor or blender. Blend to a fine purée. Spoon and scrape the mixture into a serving dish. Smooth over the top. Cover with plastic wrap and chill. Serve with buttered toast, chopped onion and capers on the side.

Guacamole Dip

2 ripe avocados
1 cup ripe tomatoes, peeled,
    seeded and chopped
½ onion, finely chopped
2 Serrano chilis, finely chopped
1 tablespoon lime juice
Salt to taste
1 tablespoon fresh cilantro,
    chopped

Mash avocados with a wooden spoon, leaving chunky. Stir in remaining ingredients. Pile on shredded iceberg lettuce or use as a dip with warmed tortilla chips.

Quick Asparagus Dip

1 can asparagus
1 cup *Homemade Mayonnaise*
Dash cayenne
Dash onion juice

Drain asparagus and blend with mayonnaise, cayenne and onion juice. Serve with corn or potato chips.

Tomato Croustades

18 slices white sandwich bread
3 tomatoes, peeled and chopped
Salt and pepper to taste
3 teaspoons fresh basil or 1½
    teaspoons dried basil
¾ cup Gruyére cheese, freshly
    grated
4 tablespoons butter, cut into bits

Cut crusts off bread and press each slice into 1 section of a greased muffin tin. Bake in 450° oven about 10 minutes or until well browned. Cool and store. (May be frozen to be used later.) Season chopped tomatoes and fill each croustade with tomato mixture. Sprinkle with Gruyére cheese and place under broiler until hot. Serve immediately.

BREADS

Everyone who has ever eaten a meal with Herbert Thomas knew that he would not take a bite of food until he saw there was hot bread on the table—and it had better be homemade!

12-Minute Cheese Biscuits
About 24 biscuits

2 cups flour
½ pound butter
½ teaspoon salt
⅛ teaspoon cayenne
½ pound cheddar cheese, grated
2 cups Rice Crispies
Dash paprika
Dash Worcestershire sauce
White of 1 egg, beaten

Mix flour, butter, salt and cayenne. Stir in cheese, Rice Crispies, paprika, Worcestershire sauce and egg white. Roll out to a thickness of about ⅓ inch and cut into rounds with a biscuit cutter. Or pinch off pieces of dough about the size of a quarter. Space biscuits evenly on a buttered cookie sheet. Bake at 350° 12 minutes.

Bacon Spoon Bread
Serves 6

¾ cups cornmeal
1½ cups cold water
2 cups sharp cheddar cheese, shredded
¼ cup soft butter or margarine
2 cloves garlic, crushed
½ teaspoon salt
1 cup milk
4 well beaten egg yolks
½ pound bacon, crisp-cooked and drained
4 stiffly beaten egg whites

Combine cornmeal and water; cook, stirring constantly, until the consistency of mush. Remove from heat; add cheese, butter, garlic and salt. Stir to melt cheese. Gradually add milk. Stir in egg yolks. Crumble bacon, reserving some for garnish if desired, and add to cornmeal mixture. Fold in egg whites. Pour into greased 2-quart soufflé dish or casserole. Bake in slow oven 325° about 65 minutes or until done. Spoon into warm dishes; top with butter and serve with spoons.

Bacon Spoon Bread is a hearty main dish soufflé that makes a simple supper with a salad and fruit. It is also good for a breakfast party.

Mexican Corn Bread
Serves 10 to 12

½ cup vegetable shortening or oil
1½ cups yellow cornmeal
1½ cups flour
½ teaspoon salt
1½ tablespoons baking powder
2 teaspoons sugar
2½ cups milk
3 eggs
1 cup yellow cream corn
1¼ cups mild cheddar cheese, shredded
¼ cup Jalapeno pepper, finely chopped
½ cup sweet red pepper, chopped
1 large white onion, finely chopped
1 clove garlic, minced
¼ pound crisply cooked bacon, finely crumbled

Preheat oven to 375°. Melt shortening in a 9×13-inch ovenproof glass baking pan, coating the bottom and sides of pan. Mix remaining ingredients in the order listed. Add the hot oil from the pan. Stir until smooth. Pour into greased pan and bake 35 to 40 minutes until golden brown.

Dutch Apple Bread
Makes 1 loaf

½ cup butter
1 cup sugar
2 large eggs
1 teaspoon vanilla extract
2 cups flour
½ teaspoon salt
⅓ cup sour milk or orange juice
1 cup apples, peeled and chopped
⅓ cup chopped walnuts

Cream the butter and sugar. Add the eggs and vanilla and beat. Add dry ingredients alternately with the sour milk or orange juice, and fold in the apples and nuts. Bake in a buttered loaf pan in a 350° oven 55 minutes, or until a broom straw comes out clean.

This delicious bread freezes well. I like to slice it thin and serve it with whipped cream cheese. The addition of ⅓ cup chopped cranberries is a taste sensation. Some good cooks sprinkle the top of the bread with a Streusel (a mixture of flour, sugar, butter, cinnamon and nuts) before baking.

Orange Nut Bread
Makes 1 loaf

2 cups flour
1¼ cups sugar
4 teaspoons baking powder
½ teaspoon salt
1¼ cups nuts
1¼ cups orange peel, cut fine
2 eggs
2 cups milk
4 tablespoons shortening, melted

Sift dry ingredients together. Add chopped nuts and orange peel. Beat eggs, add milk and melted shortening. Mix carefully. Turn into buttered bread pan and bake 1¼ hours at 375°.

Date and Nut Bread
Makes 1 loaf

1 teaspoon soda
1 box dates, cut in pieces
1 cup boiling water
1 tablespoon butter
1 cup sugar
1 egg
2 cups flour
1 teaspoon salt
1 cup pecans, chopped
1 teaspoon vanilla

Sprinkle soda over date pieces, pour boiling water over them. Cream butter and sugar, and mix in the egg. When dates are cool, combine these 2 mixtures. Add flour, salt, pecans and vanilla. Bake 1 hour at 350°.

Buttermilk Pancakes

3 eggs
2 cups buttermilk
2 cups all–purpose flour
2 teaspoons baking powder
¾ teaspoon soda
6 tablespoons melted butter
¼ teaspoon salt

Heat a lightly greased griddle until drops of water sizzle on it. Separate eggs. Beat yolks. Add 1 cup buttermilk. Sift dry ingredients, add to yolks. Add other cup buttermilk, butter and stiffly beaten whites. Pour the batter in rounds on the hot griddle. After 2 to 3 minutes when bubbles appear, turn with a spatula and bake until other side is well browned. Serve immediately with butter and hot maple syrup.

Pecan Waffles
Makes 6

2 cups flour
½ teaspoon salt
2 teaspoons baking powder
¼ to ½ teaspoon soda
2 cups buttermilk
4 to 6 tablespoons melted
   shortening
2 eggs, separated
2 tablespoons sugar
3 cups pecans, broken into
   quarters and halves

Sift dry ingredients except pecans into a bowl. Add egg yolks to the dry mixture, then add buttermilk and melted shortening. Beat egg whites until stiff. Using the same beater, beat the other mixture until smooth. Fold in the egg whites. Pour into a hot waffle iron, sprinkle ½ cup pecans onto batter and bake until well browned. Makes 6 waffles.

Herbert Thomas loved *Pecan Waffles* and wanted them at least once a week for breakfast. They are popular at the Inn.

Buttermilk Biscuits
Makes about 24 biscuits

2 cups flour
2 teaspoons baking powder
½ teaspoon salt
⅛ teaspoon soda
⅔ cups vegetable shortening
1 cup buttermilk

Combine dry ingredients and cut in shortening. Add buttermilk. Knead 3 to 4 minutes. Roll to ¼ inch thickness. Cut in rounds with cutter not more than 1½ inches in diameter. Bake at 425° until brown on top and bottom.

EGG, CHEESE AND PASTA DISHES

Cheese Grits
Serves 6 to 8

4 cups cooked grits
2 cups milk
2 tablespoons butter
4 eggs
2 teaspoons salt
½ teaspoon paprika
1 cup grated cheddar cheese

Stir milk into grits with butter, beaten eggs, salt and paprika. Add grated cheese and mix well. Turn into greased 4-cup ring mold. Bake at 350° 25 minutes until firm. Turn out on serving plate.

Pizza Supper Pie
Serves 6

1 baked pie shell
½ pound bulk pork sausage
¾ cup onion, chopped
½ teaspoon pepper
4 eggs
½ cup milk
1 cup cheddar cheese, shredded
⅔ cup pizza sauce

Slowly brown sausage and onions, breaking up sausage with a fork. Drain off fat. Add seasonings. Beat eggs and milk. Stir in sausage and cheese. Pour into baked pie shell. Bake at 325° 20 minutes or until knife inserted in center comes out clean. Spread top with pizza sauce and serve immediately.

Vermicelli Angelo
Serves 8

10 ounces vermicelli
8 eggs
1 tablespoon butter
1 clove garlic, minced
1 tablespoon onion, chopped
2 heaping teaspoons parsley,
    chopped
1 teaspoon salt
¼ teaspoon pepper
¾ cup Parmesan cheese, freshly
    grated

Drop vermicelli in a pot of boiling water with a few drops of oil and cook from 5 to 10 minutes. Break eggs into a bowl and beat until frothy. Melt butter in frying pan on low heat and add garlic, onion, parsley, salt and pepper. Pour eggs into this mixture, and then the cheese. This is the tricky part of the dish, as the eggs must NOT cook. If they do, the dish becomes a fancy scrambled egg number. As soon as the cheese melts, drain the vermicelli and add it to the hot cheese and egg mixture and stir as you would a salad, lifting it up with a spoon and fork. After it is well mixed, serve on spaghetti plates and bring out the salad bowl.

This dish must be prepared just before eating.

Welsh Rarebit Sandwich
Makes 2

1 tablespoon butter
4 teaspoons cornstarch
2 cups thin cream
2 pounds Monterey Jack cheese,
    grated
½ teaspoon salt
1 teaspoon dry mustard
¼ teaspoon cayenne
Dash Worcestershire sauce
2 Holland Rusks
2 slices tomato, peeled
4 slices crisp bacon
2 green scallions, chopped
1 tablespoon chutney, chopped

Melt butter, add cornstarch and stir well. Add cream gradually, stirring, and cook in top of double boiler 4 minutes. Add cheese, stir until it is melted and season. Place a Holland Rusk on each plate and cover with sliced tomato, salt, pepper and crisp bacon. Cover with hot Welsh rarebit and sprinkle scallions on top. Dollop with a little chutney and serve.

Blender Crêpes
Makes 12 to 14 crêpes

1½ cups milk
3 eggs
1 cup flour
Dash of salt

Blend all ingredients at top speed 30 seconds. Scrape sides of blender and blend again 15 seconds. Batter should be consistency of thick cream. Cover and refrigerate 1 to 2 hours before cooking. Grease crêpe skillet with clarified butter, leaving only the barest film of oil in the skillet. Preheat skillet until it is very hot, not smoking. Remove from heat, hold pan in air and pour in 2 tablespoons batter. Immediately tip the skillet in all directions so that the surface is evenly coated with the batter. Return the pan to medium heat and cook on 1 side 1 minute. Turn and cook on the other side 20 to 30 seconds. The second side must be used as the inside of the crêpe.

These may be made ahead of time and stored in the refrigerator tightly wrapped for up to 48 hours. They may also be frozen if they are properly wrapped. They will separate easily if first allowed to thaw completely.

Hot Crab Meat Mornay
Serves 4

1 pound lump crab meat
1 stick butter
1 bunch green onions, chopped
2 tablespoons flour
1¾ cups half-and-half
3½ cups grated Swiss or Gruyére cheese
Dash of cayenne pepper or Tabasco sauce
1 teaspoon dry mustard
1 teaspoon dry sherry
English muffins

Melt butter, sauté onions, blend in flour, cream and cheese slowly while stirring. Add seasoning except sherry. Gently fold in crab meat. Stir until mixture is hot. Blend in sherry. Spread on muffins and bake at 400° until bubbly—about 10 minutes. A pastry shell could substitute for the muffin.

This is a delicious brunch dish.

Purée of Split Pea Soup
Serves 6

1 cup dried split peas
4 cups cold water
Ham hock or ends of baked ham
2 tablespoons onion, chopped
½ cup celery, chopped
1 teaspoon pickling spice (in cloth bag)
Salt and pepper to taste
1 bay leaf
¼ teaspoon thyme
1 cup half-and-half
Dash of cayenne pepper

Soak peas overnight, wash and drain. Add to the water with ham hock, onion, celery, pickling spice, salt, pepper, bay leaf and thyme. Cook until tender. Remove pickling spices and bay leaves. Remove ham and strain through a sieve or blend in a food processor until creamy. Add cream and mix well. Reheat and add chopped ham cayenne. Serve hot with croutons on top sprinkled with paprika.

Ham and split peas make a wonderful combination, and a very satisfying dish.

Potato Soup
Serves 4

3 potatoes, peeled and sliced
1 quart milk
1 bay leaf
4 slices bacon, diced
¼ cup onion, diced
3 tablespoons butter
Salt
White pepper
1 teaspoon boveril

Boil potatoes in water until very soft. Heat milk with bay leaf until scalding. Remove bay leaf and drain potatoes. Put potatoes and hot milk in blender or food processor until smooth. Put in double boiler.

Sauté bacon until crisp. Add onion and sauté until soft. Add to blended potato mixture with butter, salt and pepper to taste. Add boveril and serve steaming hot.

Cream of Corn Soup
Serves 6

2 strips bacon, finely chopped
2 tablespoons onion, finely
    chopped
2 cups fresh or frozen corn
2 tablespoons butter
2 tablespoons flour
3½ cups milk
3½ cups light cream
1 teaspoon salt
½ teaspoon pepper
½ teaspoon sugar
1 bay leaf

Fry bacon until crisp; add onion and sauté until soft. Quickly blend corn in food processor and add to bacon and onions in skillet. Cook until corn begins to brown. Add butter and then flour. Cook slowly 3 minutes. Add milk, salt, pepper, bay leaf and sugar. Stir and cook until thickened, then add cream and heat until smooth. Serve with hot crackers.

An elegant soup—and one my husband liked especially.

Barley Soup
Serves 4

¼ cup pearl barley
1 pint boiling water
¼ teaspoon salt
1 quart beef soup stock
½ cup celery, diced
1 cup cream
½ tablespoon boveril

Wash barley in cold water and drain. Cook in boiling, salted water until tender, 2 hours or more. When water has evaporated, add beef soup stock. (Canned consommé may be substituted for fresh beef stock.) Add celery and cook until tender. Add cream and boveril, stir and serve hot with *Croutons.*

Rich Oyster Stew
Serves 4 to 6

¼ cup butter
2 onions, sliced
1 clove garlic, slivered
1 carrot sliced
1 stalk celery, sliced
1 teaspoon chopped parsley
¼ teaspoon thyme

Melt butter in a large, heavy saucepan. Add onions, garlic, carrot celery, parsley and thyme. Cover and cook over a moderate heat about 10 minutes. Add milk, cream and oyster liquor. Heat to boiling point but do not boil. Strain into another saucepan. Add oysters and heat only until oysters curl at the edges. Season with salt, pepper, Worcestershire sauce and asco sauce. Ladle into hot soup bowls and serve with heated crackers or crusty French bread.

1 ½ cups milk
1 ½ cups heavy cream
24 oysters in their liquor
1 teaspoon salt
Few grinds fresh pepper
Dash Worcestershire sauce
Dash Tabasco sauce

Oyster stew makes a wonderful winters' night meal.

Creole Gumbo
Serves 4 to 6

4 thick slices bacon, cut up
3 tablespoons flour
1 cup celery, diced
1 medium green pepper, coarsely
   chopped
1 onion, peeled and chopped
2 cloves garlic, minced
1 #2 can tomatoes with juice
1 bay leaf
1 cup beef consommé
1 cup water
3 hard shell crabs, cleaned, boiled
   and halved
1 cup okra, sliced
1 pound raw shrimp, shelled
½ pound crab meat
1 dozen oysters, shucked, with
   liquid
Gumbo filé
1 jalapeño pepper

Cook bacon in large kettle until fat has been rendered. Remove bacon and set aside. Lower heat and add flour slowly stirring into bacon fat. Cook until dark brown, taking care not to scorch roux. Add celery, peppers, onion and garlic and cook until garlic is brown. Add tomatoes and juice, consommé and water. Add cooked bacon, crabs, salt and pepper and simmer 1 hour. Add okra and simmer 15 minutes longer. Add shrimp, crab meat and oysters with their liquor and simmer 15 minutes. Just before serving add filé to taste (1 teaspoon per quart). Do not boil after adding filé. Serve hot over rice in a bowl.

Jim Thomas brought this gumbo recipe back from New Orleans. He likes to serve it in covered bowls to keep it piping hot.

French Onion Soup
Serves 6

¼ cup butter
1 pound onions, thinly sliced
¾ teaspoon paprika
¼ cup vegetable oil
⅓ cup flour
3 cups beef stock
¼ teaspoon celery salt
Salt and pepper to taste
1 tablespoon cognac
1½ cups *Croutons*
½ pound Gruyére or Swiss cheese

Melt the butter, add onion and cook over low heat until the onions are caramel colored. Add the paprika. Make the roux by browning the oil and flour mixed, being certain it is evenly browned. Add the onions, roux, celery salt, salt and pepper to the beef stock in a large saucepan and stir until it boils. Let simmer at least 1 hour. Add cognac and pour hot soup into warmed ovenproof bowls. Add croutons and lay two slices of cheese crosswise over each bowl, making certain that some cheese extends beyond the bowl on all sides. Place under the broiler and heat until cheese is bubbling and has run over the sides of the bowl.

Brie cheese is also wonderful melted over onion soup.

Argolemono Soup
Serves 6

6 cups chicken broth
¼ cup raw rice
1 teaspoon salt
3 eggs
¼ cup fresh lemon juice
1 lemon, thinly sliced
Paprika

Combine chicken broth, rice and salt in a large saucepan. Bring to a boil and reduce the heat, cover and simmer until the rice is just tender (15 to 20 minutes). Remove pan from heat. Beat eggs in a bowl until fluffy and beat in lemon juice. Slowly stir about two cups of the hot broth into the egg–lemon mixture and whisk vigorously. Pour this mixture back into the rest of the soup. Whisk it until slightly thickened. Cool to room temperature, then refrigerate until icy cold. The soup will thicken and settle somewhat as it chills. Stir before serving and garnish with lemon slices and paprika.

Argolemono is a refreshing Greek soup.

Crème Vichyssoise
Serves 6 to 8

6 leeks (white part only)
2 medium onions
¼ pound butter
¾ pound potatoes, peeled
2 quarts chicken stock
Salt and white pepper
1 cup half-and-half
Chives

Chop leeks and onions and sauté until soft in butter. Add stock and potatoes cut into small pieces. Add salt and pepper to taste and cook until potatoes are done. Blend in a food processor. Add cream and chill thoroughly. Garnish with chopped chives and serve.

Gazpacho
Serves 4

1 clove garlic
2 cucumbers, peeled and seeded
1 green pepper, seeded
1 teaspoon wine vinegar
½ teaspoon olive oil
2 cups tomato juice
4 tomatoes, peeled
Salt and cayenne pepper
Cumin powder
Dash of Worcestershire sauce

Place all ingredients in blender or food processor and coarsely blend. Serve very cold with tray of chopped tomatoes, chopped cucumbers, chopped onions and chopped pepper.

Herbert and I brought the *Gazpacho* recipe home from Sevilla, Spain where I first tasted it in 1963. It is refreshing on a hot day.

Tomato Madrilene
Serves 6 to 8

3 tablespoons unflavored gelatin
¼ cup cold water, consommé or tomato juice
2 cups tomato juice
2 cups chicken broth
Salt and pepper
Garlic salt
Sour cream
Caviar

Soften gelatin in cold liquid in sauce pan and heat until completely dissolved. Add tomato juice, chicken broth, salt, pepper and garlic salt, season and strain. Chill. Break up with fork or cut in cubes and served piled in bouillon cups. Garnish with sour cream and caviar.

Jellied Clam and Beef Broth
Serves 4

2 ½ cups fish stock or clam juice
2 cups beef consommé
½ cup dry white wine
½ cup water
1 tablespoon unflavored gelatin
¼ cup cold water
Sour cream
Chopped chives
Lemon slices

Pour beef and clam broths, wine and water into saucepan. Simmer about 5 minutes. Soften gelatin in cold water and stir into hot broth until dissolved. Chill until jelled. Serve in chilled cups and garnish with sour cream/chives dollop into which you have placed ½ of a thin lemon slice.

Wonderful in hot weather!

SALADS

Artichoke Crab Salad
Serves 6

1 cup lump crab meat, flaked
1 cup celery, diced
1 tablespoon capers
1 tablespoon lemon juice
¼ cup mayonnaise
12 canned artichoke hearts,
    drained
Dash cayenne
Dash paprika

Combine crab, celery, capers, lemon juice and mayonnaise. Place on a bed of curly lettuce. Drain artichoke hearts. Cut each heart in fourths and open like a flower. Marinate in your favorite vinaigrette dressing. Garnish each serving with 2 hearts, a dollop of mayonnaise and paprika.

Avocado Mousse
Serves 16

1 tablespoon gelatin
2 tablespoons cold water
1 package lemon jello
2 cups hot water
Salt to taste
1 cup mashed avocado
½ cup heavy cream, whipped
1 tablespoon lemon juice

Soften gelatin in cold water. Add jello and pour boiling water over all. Stir well and set in refrigerator. When partially congealed, stir in remaining ingredients. Pour into a mold lightly greased with salad oil and set in refrigerator. Fresh fruits make a nice garnish.

Avocado with Lobster Salad
Serves 6

3 medium avocados
1 tablespoon lemon juice
1 clove garlic
6 ounces lobster meat
1 cup celery, chopped
2 green onions, chopped
1 teaspoon Worcestershire sauce
2 eggs, hard-boiled and chopped
½ cup mayonnaise
1 tomato, peeled and cut in wedges
1 tablespoon *Oil and Vinegar Dressing*

Peel avocados, cut in half. Remove seed and rub surface with lemon juice and bruised garlic. Break up lobster into chunks and mix with celery, onions, Worcestershire sauce, eggs and mayonnaise. Spoon into cavities of avocados and serve on crisp, shredded lettuce, garnished with quarters of fresh peeled tomatoes which have been sprinkled with *Oil and Vinegar Dressing*. Serve with a dollop of mayonnaise and dash of paprika on top.

If fresh lobster is not available, canned lobster will substitute.

Curried Chicken Salad
Serves 6 to 8

CURRY MAYONNAISE:
½ cup mayonnaise
2 teaspoons curry powder
1 tablespoon fresh ginger, chopped
   (or preserved ginger)
1 teaspoon grated onion
½ teaspoon salt
½ cup heavy cream, whipped

Combine mayonnaise, curry powder, ginger, onion and salt. Mix well. Fold in cream and refrigerate until needed.

CHICKEN SALAD:
2 cups cooked chicken (or turkey), cubed
¼ cup *Oil and Vinegar Dressing*
2 cups fresh pineapple, cut in small chunks
   (or 1 pound 4½-ounce can pineapple chunks, well drained)

In a large bowl combine chicken and *Oil and Vinegar Dressing*, tossing until well coated. Refrigerate, covered, at least 2 hours. Add pineapple, apple, grapes, chutney and green pepper to chicken and mix well. Gently fold in curry mayonnaise until well blended. Refrigerate, covered, until chilled, about 2 hours. To serve, arrange lettuce on platter and mound salad in center. Garnish with watercress.

1 ½ cups large apple, pared and
  diced
1 ½ cup seedless white grapes
¼ cup chutney, chopped
¼ cup green pepper, chopped
Crisp lettuce

Crab Meat Salad
Serves 4

1 cup lump crab meat
1 teaspoon grated onion
¼ cup *Oil and Vinegar Dressing*
1 cup celery, chopped
¼ cup mayonnaise
1 tablespoon capers, optional
Bibb or curly lettuce
Avocado slices or tomato quarters

Drain crab and check for bone and cartilege. Add onion and marinate in oil and vinegar dressing. Chill 1 hour. Combine with celery, mayonnaise and capers. Heap on bed of lettuce and garnish with avocado or tomato.

Pasta Shrimp Salad
Serves 4

1 cup mayonnaise
¼ cup green onions, chopped
½ cup celery, chopped
3 tablespoons fresh parsley,
  chopped
¼ cup green pepper, chopped
1 tablespoon lemon juice
Salt and cayenne pepper to taste
Dash garlic powder
1 cup small shrimp, cleaned and
  cooked
2 cups shell pasta, cooked al dente,
  drained and cooled

Mix all ingredients except shrimp with mayonnaise. Fold in shrimp. Toss mixture with pasta and serve.

Shrimp Salad
Serves 4

2 cups shrimp, cleaned and cooked
1 cup celery, chopped
¼ cup green onions, chopped
1 tablespoon capers
3 eggs, hard-boiled and chopped
½ cup mayonnaise
1 tablespoon lemon juice
Salt and cayenne to taste
Tomato wedges
Mayonnaise for garnish

Mix lightly and serve on fluffy lettuce bed. Garnish with a large shrimp, tomato wedges and a dollop of mayonnaise.

Fresh Spinach Salad
Serves 4

1 pound fresh spinach, washed and
   dried
6 slices crisp bacon, crumbled
½ cup green onions, chopped
1 egg, hard-boiled and grated

Tear spinach and sprinkle crumbled bacon, chopped onion and egg on top. Top with dressing.

DRESSING:
1 cup olive oil
¼ cup water
½ cup vinegar
1 package Hidden Valley seasoning
1 clove garlic, crushed
½ teaspoon dill weed
Salt and freshly ground black
   pepper to taste

Add ⅓ cup crumbled blue cheese when served as a luncheon entrée.

Frozen Fruit Salad
Serves 8

2 #3 cans fruits for salads (not fruit cocktail)
3 ripe bananas
1 cup small marshmallows
1 cup mayonnaise
½ cup Durkee's dressing
1 pint heavy cream, whipped

Drain fruit and cut in smaller pieces. Slice bananas into fruit. Add marshmallows. Mix mayonnaise and Durkee's together and add to fruit mix, mixing well. Fold in whipped cream. Freeze in Pyrex baking pan or in individual containers. Serve with dainty chicken salad sandwiches, potato chips and 2 ripe olives.

Three-Tier Molded Salad
Serves 14 to 16

Make molded *Chicken Salad Supreme* with variations (include hard-boiled eggs, sliced) and leave room in a large mold for 2 more layers. Just before it is firm, cover with the next layer:

1 8-ounce package cream cheese, softened
½ cup mayonnaise
Salt and cayenne pepper to taste
¼ cup cucumber, peeled, seeded and chopped
1 tablespoon gelatin
¼ cup lemon juice

Mix cream cheese, mayonnaise, salt and pepper and cucumber well in food processor or mixer. Soften gelatin in lemon juice in small pan and place on heat to dissolve. Add to cream cheese mixture. Cool and add to *Chicken Salad* mold. Just before second layer hardens, add the *Tomato Aspic* to fill the mold and chill until firm. Unmold on bed of lettuce and serve with *Homemade Mayonnaise.*

Tomato Aspic Ring
Serves 6 to 8

2 ½ cups tomato juice
1 teaspoon parsley, chopped
1 bay leaf
1 tablespoon sugar
¼ cup celery, diced
⅛ cup onion, diced
1 teaspoon salt
4 black peppercorns
1 tablespoon vinegar
6 cloves
2 teaspoons Worcestershire sauce
2 tablespoons gelatin
1 cup cold water

Combine all ingredients except gelatin and cold water in saucepan and simmer until vegetables are soft. Soften gelatin in cold water. Add this to hot mixture, stir until dissolved. Strain. Moisten individual molds or a 1 ½-quart ring mold so the aspic will unmold easily. Pour into molds and let stand in refrigerator overnight. Serve chicken salad in center, top with dash of *Homemade Mayonnaise,* then a slice of lemon sprinkled with paprika.

This recipe may be varied in endless ways. I like to stuff canned artichoke hearts with Roquefort and cream cheese whipped together and drop them into the aspic just before it congeals. Or we sometimes drop some jumbo shrimp that have been marinated in French dressing into the mold.

Corn Bread Salad
Serves 2

3 fresh tomatoes, peeled and diced
1 cucumber, peeled and sliced
1 red onion, thinly sliced
1 garlic pod, minced
Olive oil
Dash of vinegar
Cracked pepper
Corn bread sticks, or leftover corn
  bread

Place all ingredients except corn bread in a bowl and let stand 30 minutes. Split corn bread sticks and place on plate. Generously spoon salad over corn bread and serve.

My grandson, Scott McGehee, brought this recipe back from Italy where it is a summer favorite. It is usually made with leftover stale bread. It is ideal for leftover corn bread or, still better, fresh corn bread sticks.

Dreamy Apricot Salad
Serves 10 to 12

3-ounce package apricot flavored gelatin
⅓ cup sugar
⅓ cup cold water
4¾-ounce jar apricot baby food
1 10-ounce can crushed pineapple, undrained
1 7-ounce can sweetened condensed milk, chilled
4 ounces cream cheese, softened
¾ cup chopped nuts
2 tablespoons grated orange rind

Combine gelatin, sugar and water in a small saucepan. Bring to a boil, stirring to dissolve sugar and gelatin. Remove from heat, and stir in fruit. Set aside to cool. Combine condensed milk and cream cheese, beating until smooth. Stir in gelatin mixture, then nuts and orange rind. Pour into a quart mold, and chill until firm.

Royal Anne Congealed Salad
Serves 8 to 10

2 packages lemon jello
¾ cup boiling water
1 can Royal Anne cherries
1 can pineapple chunks
Rind of 2 oranges
1½ cups water
¼ cup sugar
Dash mayonnaise
Dash paprika
Sprig of parsley
Orange sections

Dissolve jello with boiling water plus enough fruit juice to make up rest of liquid. Add cherries and pineapple, pour into ring mold and refrigerate. Boil orange peel in water and sugar until tender. Pour off the sugar and water, cut rind into slivers and mix with mayonnaise. When salad in congealed, serve garnished with orange sections and a dollop of mayonnaise mixture.

Eggs en Gelée
Serves 8

2 tablespoons unflavored gelatin
½ cup cold water
1 cup hot chicken broth
10 hard-boiled eggs, coarsely
   grated
¼ teaspoon pepper
½ cup chili sauce
½ cup mayonnaise
1 teaspoon salt
1 tablespoon grated onion

Soften gelatin in cold water, then dissolve in hot broth. Allow to cool. Combine remaining ingredients and add to gelatin mixture. Pour into oiled mold. Chill until firm. Serve on shredded lettuce with mayonnaise.

Eggs en Gelée are often a part of the Sunday buffet.

Apricots or Green Gage Plum Salad
Serves 8

1 #2 can green gage plums
1 package lime jello
1 ½ cups very hot water
½ cup plum juice
⅛ teaspoon salt
1 teaspoon vinegar
½ cup blanched, toasted almonds
1 3-ounce package cream cheese
½ teaspoon ground ginger

Drain juice from plums and reserve. Dissolve jello in water, add juice, salt and vinegar. Cool. Pit plums and insert almonds in each. Arrange in bottom of mold. Pour ½ of the jello over them and chill until firm. When rest of jello begins to thicken, whip in ginger and cream cheese and pour over plums. Chill until firm.

This is a tart salad, good with turkey or game.

Cucumber Ring with Crab Meat
Serves 4

1 tablespoon unflavored gelatin
¼ cup cold water
1 ½ cups boiling water
4 tablespoons lemon juice
¼ teaspoon salt
¼ teaspoon cayenne pepper
2 teaspoons fresh dill weed or ½
    teaspoon dried dill leaves
1 teaspoon grated onion
1 cup grated cucumber, drained
1 ½ cups lump crab meat
⅓ cup *Oil and Vinegar Dressing*

Soften gelatin in cold water and dissolve in boiling water. Add lemon juice, seasonings and onion. Chill until slightly thickened. Fold in cucumbers and pour into 4 individual ring molds or one 3-cup ring mold. Chill until congealed. Unmold and garnish with watercress. Fill center with crab meat that has been moistened with *Oil and Vinegar Dressing*. Serve with tart *Homemade Mayonnaise*.

Cool As A Cucumber Salad
Serves 6

1 3-ounce package lime gelatin
¾ cup hot water
¼ cup lemon juice
1 teaspoon onion juice
1 cup cucumber, peeled and
    chopped
6 slices canned pineapple, drained
Lettuce
½ cup sour cream
Ripe olives

Dissolve gelatin in hot water. Add lemon and onion juices. Chill until partially set. Stir in sour cream and cucumber. Pour into 6 individual molds and chill until firm. Unmold each on pineapple ring atop a ruffle of lettuce. Garnish with ripe olives.

Roquefort Dressing

⅔ cups olive oil
¼ cup vegetable oil
⅓ cup vinegar
1 teaspoon salt
1 clove garlic, finely chopped
½ cup sugar
1 tablespoon paprika
Juice of 1 lemon
½ cup Roquefort cheese, crumbled

Combine the first 8 ingredients and mix well to make 2 cups oil and vinegar dressing. Beat cheese into dressing.

Lima Bean Mélange
Serves 6

1 cup lima beans
½ cucumber
¼ cup green pepper, minced
¼ cup green onions, chopped
¼ cup celery, chopped
Salt and pepper to taste
½ teaspoon dried basil
½ teaspoon dried thyme
½ cup vinaigrette dressing
1 tablespoon mayonnaise
1½ pound fresh tomatoes, peeled
    and diced
Curly lettuce, washed, dried and
    chilled

Cook lima beans in very little water until tender, and drain. Mix with cucumbers, onion, green pepper, celery, seasonings and enough mayonnaise to moisten. Carefully fold in the diced tomatoes. Chill and serve in a lettuce-lined bowl.

Lima beans, or butter beans as we used to call them, are not in vogue these days. But I think they are a wonderfully flavored vegetable. This is a hearty enough dish as the main course at lunch or to accompany a steak broiled on the grill. If you have baby lima beans in your garden, good—otherwise, use the frozen kind as they are picked and processed before they become too mature.

M E A T

Tournedoes of Beef
Serves 4

12 to 16 ounces beef tenderloin
3 tablespoons meat glaze
½ cup Madeira wine
4 slices white sandwich bread
1 tablespoon olive oil
1 tablespoon butter
1 can pâté de foie gras (pâté of chicken livers, seasoned)
½ cup fresh mushrooms, sliced

Have the tenderloin of beef cut in ¾-inch slices at a slant to a weight of about 3 or 4 ounces. Prepare the Madeira sauce in a crêpe pan over heat. Add meat glaze with ½ cup of wine to pan and heat until it has reduced by half. Set aside. Trim bread slices to size of tournedoes and lightly fry in another small pan with olive oil and butter. Broil tournedoes 7 to 8 minutes (do not overcook) in a hot skillet. Introduce Madeira sauce, and brown meat on both sides. Place each portion of meat on brown croutons and top with pâté and sliced mushrooms.

Filet Mignon

This choice cut of meat is selected from prime U.S. beef properly aged and expertly trimmed. The sauce that follows should complement such a fine piece of meat. Broil 1 filet per person under broiler or in hot skillet until brown on the outside and rare in the center.

SAUCE BORDELAISE:
2 tablespoons shallots or green onions, finely chopped
¾ cup burgundy wine
½ bay leaf
Pinch of thyme
⅓ cup fresh mushrooms, sliced
2 tablespoons butter
1½ tablespoons flour
1 cup beef broth
Salt and pepper to taste

Mix shallots, wine, bay leaf and thyme. Simmer until wine is reduced to about ¼ cup. Strain, rubbing shallots through sieve. Sauté mushrooms in butter. Stir in flour. Add strong beef broth, and cook, stirring until mixture boils thoroughly and is clear and thickened. Add salt and pepper to taste and the wine mixture, and simmer 5 minutes. Makes about 1¼ cups of sauce.

Cannelloni
Serves 8 to 12

PASTA:

1 ½ cups unsifted all–purpose flour
2 eggs

Pour the flour into a large mixing bowl, make a well in the center and break the eggs into it. Mix together until the dough can be gathered in a rough ball. Or pasta can be mixed in a food processor. Knead the dough on a floured board, working in a little extra dough if the dough seems sticky. Wrap it in plastic wrap and let dough rest at least 10 minutes before rolling.

Divide dough into 2 balls. Place 1 ball on a floured board and flatten it with the palm of your hand into an oblong about 1 inch thick. Dust the top lightly with flour. Then, using a heavy rolling pin, start at one end of the oblong and roll it out lengthwise away from you to within an inch or so of the farthest edge. Turn the dough crosswise and roll across its width. Repeat, turning and rolling the dough, until it is paper thin. (If you have a pasta maker, all of the kneading and rolling can be done in the machine). Cut into about 36 rectangles of 2×3 inches. Bring 6 to 8 quarts of water, to which salt and a few drops of olive oil have been added, to a boil in a large kettle. Drop in the pieces of pasta and stir gently with a wooden spoon for a few moments. Return the water to a boil and cook over high heat 5 minutes. Drain, cool slightly, then spread the pasta pieces side by side on paper towels to dry.

FILLING:

2 tablespoons olive oil
¼ cup onion, finely chopped
1 teaspoon garlic, finely chopped
1 10-ounce package frozen chopped spinach
2 tablespoons butter
1 pound round steak, ground twice
2 chicken livers
5 tablespoons Parmesan cheese, freshly grated
2 tablespoons heavy cream
2 eggs, lightly beaten
½ teaspoon dried oregano
Salt and freshly ground pepper to taste

In a heavy skillet, sauté the onions and garlic in olive oil until soft. Defrost and squeeze spinach dry; stir into skillet and cook, stirring constantly, until moisture has evaporated. Transfer to a large mixing bowl. Melt 1 tablespoon butter in the same skillet and lightly brown the ground meat, stirring constantly to break up lumps. Add the meat to the spinach mixture. Melt 1 more tablespoon butter in skillet and cook the livers, turning them frequently, 3 to 4 minutes, until they are somewhat firm, lightly browned but still pink inside. Chop them coarsely. Then add them to the mixture in the bowl along with Parmesan, cream, eggs and oregano. With a wooden spoon mix ingredients together, gently but thoroughly. Taste and season with salt and pepper.

BESCIAMELLA SAUCE:
¼ cup butter or margarine
½ cup all–purpose flour
1 cup milk
1 cup light cream
Salt and white pepper to taste

In a heavy saucepan, melt butter over moderate heat. Remove the pan from heat and stir in the flour. Pour in milk and cream all at once, whisking constantly until the flour is partially dissolved. Return the pan to high heat and cook, stirring constantly with the whisk. When the sauce comes to a boil and is smooth, reduce the heat. Simmer, stirring until sauce is thick enough to coat the whisk heavily. Remove from heat, and season with salt and pepper.

TOMATO SAUCE:
4 tablespoons olive oil
1 cup onions, finely chopped
1 stalk celery, finely chopped
4 cups Italian plum tomatoes,
  coarsely chopped but not drained
6 tablespoons tomato paste
2 tablespoons fresh basil, minced
  or 1 tablespoon dried basil
2 teaspoons sugar
1 teaspoon salt
Freshly ground black pepper

Heat olive oil in a 2– to 3-quart saucepan, add onions and cook until soft. Add tomatoes, tomato paste, basil, sugar, salt and pepper. Reduce heat to low and simmer, with the pan partially covered, about 40 minutes. Stir occasionally. Blend sauce in a food processor or strain through a sieve.

TOPPING:
3 cups tomato sauce
2 tablespoons freshly grated
  Parmesan cheese
2 tablespoons butter, cut in pieces

Preheat oven to 375°. Place a tablespoon or so of the filling on the bottom third of each of the pasta rectangles and roll them up. Pour a little of the tomato sauce into two 10×14-inch shallow baking dishes or 1 larger one. Lay the cannelloni side by side in 1 layer on the tomato sauce. Pour the besciamella over it and spoon the rest of the tomato sauce on top. Scatter in 2 tablespoons of grated cheese and dot with 2 tablespoons of butter. Bake cannelloni uncovered 20 minutes or until cheese is melted and the sauce bubbling. Slide the baking dishes under a hot broiler 30 seconds to brown the top. Serve the cannelloni directly from the baking dish.

For chicken or turkey cannelloni, substitute 2 cups of cooked chicken or turkey, coarsely chopped, for the ground beef in the filling. A delicious vegetarian version substitutes 2 cups ricotta cheese for the ground beef and chicken livers.

I first tasted Cannelloni at the Hosteria del Orso in Rome, a beautiful and very old inn where Dante once stayed. It is a wonderfully light Italian dish that can be frozen and served to a large crowd with a salad, fruit compote and French bread. It's worth the trouble!

Beef Burgundy
Serves 6

2 ½ pounds chuck beef, cut into large cubes
Flour for coating beef
2 tablespoons olive oil
2 tablespoons butter
2 tablespoons warmed cognac
2 slices bacon
2 cloves of garlic
1 large carrot
1 large leek
2 medium onions, coarsely chopped
1 tablespoon parsley, chopped
2 bay leaves
½ teaspoon thyme
½ bottle Burgundy
½ pound mushroom caps
2 teaspoons flour
2 teaspoons butter
1 small lemon
1 pound pearl onions
Pinch of sugar
1 teaspoon olive oil
1 teaspoon butter

Dredge beef cubes in flour, then brown on all sides in a skillet over high heat in butter and olive oil. Sprinkle the meat with salt and pepper, pour over it warmed cognac and ignite the spirit. When the flame dies, transfer the meat into a large casserole.

To the skillet add bacon, garlic, carrot, leek, onions and parsley, all coarsely chopped. Cook, stirring until the bacon is crisp and the vegetables are lightly browned. Transfer the vegetable mixture to the casserole and add bay leaf, thyme and burgundy, saving a little to add to the pearl onions. Add enough water to cover the meat. Cook the beef in a moderate oven (350°) 1 to 1 ½ hours. Stir in bit by bit flour mixed into a paste with butter and cook the meat for approximately 2 hours or until tender.

Brown pearl onions in butter with a sprinkling of sugar. Add a little burgundy, cover and cook about 15 minutes, or until the onions are almost tender. Sauté mushroom caps in a little butter and olive oil until they are lightly browned on one side. Sprinkle them with lemon juice and turn them to brown the other side. Keep them warm, but do not cover.

To serve, add the onions to the casserole, arrange the mushroom caps on top and sprinkle with finely chopped parsley.

Beef Burgundy is a hearty winter dish.

Roast Leg of Fresh Pork
Serves 3 to 4 persons per pound

1 12– to 14-pound fresh ham,
   boned and trimmed
¼ cup salt
¼ teaspoon each ground allspice,
   bay leaf, paprika, sage and thyme
1 teaspoon freshly ground
   peppercorns
½ cup cooking oil
1 large onion and carrot, chopped
5 large unpeeled garlic cloves
2 ribs of celery
¼ cup flour
2 cups chicken broth
2 cups white wine
2 medium tomatoes, chopped
Herb bouquet of 6 parsley sprigs, 1
   bay leaf and ½ teaspoon each
   sage and thyme

Purchase the fresh ham boned and trussed appropriately. Make a marinade of salt, allspice, bay leaf, paprika, sage, thyme and peppercorns. Rub in mixture all over the inside flesh of the ham. Place the meat in a plastic bag and refrigerate 2 days. If you do not have time to refrigerate, leave in marinade as long as possible.

Preheat the oven to 425°. Dry the meat thoroughly with paper towels, brush it all over with cooking oil, set on a rack in a roasting pan and place in the middle level of the oven. Roast 15 minutes, rapidly basting twice with cooking oil. Turn oven down to 350°, and continue roasting, basting exposed flesh every 20 minutes with the marinade and the fat accumulated in the pan. After 2 hours, add chopped onion and carrot and the large unpeeled garlic cloves.

The roast is done at a meat thermometer reading of 155 to 160°. Let it rest 20 minutes before carving. (This allows the juices to retreat back into the flesh.)

For the sauce, if you have the rind and the bone, you can put them into the oven at 450° with the chopped carrot and onion and a sprinkling of olive oil and use this for a base. If you do not have these, use drippings from roast, work in flour and brown 10 minutes. Transfer to a saucepan, adding garlic and celery. Blend in chicken broth, pour white wine into the browning pan, set over heat and scrape up coagulated juices into the liquid; scrape into the saucepan along with enough water, if needed, to cover ingredients by 1½ inches. Bring to a simmer, add tomatoes and an herb bouquet. Cover loosely and simmer 30 minutes, skimming occasionally and adding more water if liquid evaporates below level of ingredients. Strain, pressing juices out of vegetables. Heat and serve with the roast leg of fresh pork.

Baked Ham Eden Isle

3 to 4 servings per pound

1 large cooked ham (12 to 15 pounds)
¾ cup brown sugar
3 tablespoons brandy
1 jar apricot marmalade
1 tablespoon dry mustard

Bake ham according to directions. An hour before it is done, remove the rind and score the fat in diamonds or squares, and sprinkle it with brown sugar and brandy. Pour into the pan the apricot marmalade and dry mustard. Finish roasting the ham, basting often with the syrup. Serve hot.

Ham Loaf

Serves 8

2½ pounds beef and ham, ground
Salt and pepper to taste
2 cloves garlic, pressed or chopped extra fine
1 cup beef stock to scald meat
1 tablespoon Dijon mustard
1 egg
¾ cup cracker crumbs

Mix all ingredients. Shape into loaf and pat with brown sugar to crisp top. Let mellow, if possible 1 hour. Bake uncovered 30 minutes then cover with foil and bake another 1½ hours, at about 300°.

This is a good way to use leftover ham.

French Style Boneless Leg of Lamb

3 to 4 servings per pound

1 bonelesss fresh lamb leg, netted, or rolled and tied (about 5 pounds)
1½ cup fresh mushrooms, finely chopped
1 teaspoon butter
½ cup onions, finely chopped
4 ounces boiled ham, diced
¼ cup finely chopped parsley
1 tablespoon thyme leaves
6 garlic cloves

If boneless leg is not purchased netted and tied, sprinkle inside with salt and pepper. Then fill with ham–mushroom mixture and net or tie. For ham–mushroom stuffing, sauté mushrooms and onions in butter about 5 minutes. Toss with diced ham, parsley and thyme. If lamb is already netted or tied, make incisions with a sharp knife 2 to 3 inches deep between netting. Using fingers, pack ham–mushroom mixture into cuts in rows along top until all is used. Insert cloves of garlic (cut in half) at random just under the skin. Bake the boned stuffed lamb 15 to 20 minutes in hot oven (425°) to start browning; reduce heat to 325° and continue baking about 60 minutes or to 140° on meat thermometer for

medium rare, 160° for well-done. Season with salt and pepper and let rest 15 minutes before carving. Skim fat from drippings and add pan liquid to make *French Sauce.*

FRENCH SAUCE:

1 ½ **cups beef broth**
½ **cup onion, finely chopped**
½ **cup carrots, finely chopped**
½ **cup celery, finely chopped**
1 **cup dry red wine**
1 **tablespoon parsley sprigs**
1 **small can tomato paste**
1 **bay leaf**
½ **teaspoon thyme**

Combine all ingredients and simmer 30 minutes. Strain through fine sieve.

Irish Lamb Stew
Serves 6 to 8

3 **tablespoons vegetable oil**
3 **tablespoons butter**
5 **pounds lamb shoulder, boned and**
  trimmed
4 **cups lamb or veal stock**
1 **medium-sized onion, quartered**
Salt and pepper to taste
2 **ounces Scotch (optional)**
5 **potatoes, peeled and quartered**
5 **carrots, peeled and cut in pieces**
2 **turnips, peeled and quartered**
  (optional)
1 **pint pearl onions, trimmed**
½ **teaspoon dried sage**
¼ **cup chopped parsley**
2 **tablespoons sugar**

Cut lamb into 1– to 2-inch cubes and brown in the oil and 2 tablespoons butter in a heavy Dutch oven. Remove meat and brown the vegetables in the oil. Remove vegetables and reserve. Pour off the oil and add the stock to the pan. Bring to a boil and deglaze pan by scraping brown bits from the bottom. Add meat and seasonings back to the pan, cover tightly and simmer slowly about 1½ hours or until meat is tender. Skim off the fat and thicken with the roux. Add potatoes and carrots to the pan and simmer until they are tender. Meanwhile boil the pearl onions in lightly salted water until tender (about 8 minutes). Boil the turnip wedges in lightly salted water about 4 minutes. In a medium skillet melt the remaining 2 tablespoons butter and add the onions and turnips. Sprinkle with the sugar and cook until they are golden and caramelized, turning often. Add these to the stew and serve on heated plates.

This is a variation of the delicious Irish stew we have enjoyed so much in Ireland.

Veal Scallopini with Marsala
Serves 2

½ **pound veal scallopini, cut into**
  ¼-inch slices
2 **tablespoons butter**
2 **tablespoons olive oil**
¼ **cup Marsala**

OPTIONAL:

½ **cup mushrooms, sliced**
¼ **cup green peppers, chopped**
¼ **cup onions, chopped**
¼ **cup celery, chopped**
4 **ounces tomatoes, chopped**

Cut the veal into pieces measuring about 3×3 inches or larger. Place them between sheets of wax paper and pound lightly to flatten, using the bottom of a heavy skillet or a flat mallet.

Blend the flour with salt and pepper and dredge the meat to coat lightly. In a large, heavy skillet, heat the butter and oil and when it is very hot, but not brown, add the meat in 1 layer. Cook over relatively high heat until brown on one side. Turn and cook until golden brown on the other. The cooking time should be from 4 to 6 minutes.

Transfer the meat to 2 plates and keep warm. To the skillet add the wine and stir to dissolve the particles in the pan. Reduce wine slightly and pour equal amounts over each serving. Or add optional ingredients to the sauce and simmer briefly before serving.

CHICKEN

Chicken Breasts with Tarragon
Serves 6

6 chicken breasts, boned, skinned and halved
Salt and pepper
¼ cup flour
¼ cup butter
1 tablespoon shallots, chopped
¼ cup dry vermouth or other dry white wine
1 teaspoon chopped fresh tarragon or 1/2 teaspoon dried tarragon
¼ cup chicken broth
¼ cup heavy cream

Salt and pepper the breasts and dredge them in flour. Save the remaining flour for later. Heat 3 tablespoons of the butter in a big, heavy skillet and drop in the chicken, browning it briefly on both sides. Remove the chicken to a hot plate to keep warm. Add the shallots and sauté them 1 or 2 minutes.

Pour the wine into the skillet and turn up heat. Cook liquid until it is reduced by more than half, scraping up the brown particles left from the chicken. Add the remaining flour and stir to make a thick paste. Add the tarragon and stir. Pour in the broth and continue stirring. Put the chicken back in the skillet, lower the heat, cover and cook until the meat is tender—probably about 25 minutes.

Remove chicken. Add cream to broth mixture and heat to serve over chicken.

Chicken Divan
Serves 4

2 pounds chicken breast, cooked and sliced
1 large bunch broccoli, trimmed and steamed
2 cups *Hollandaise Sauce*
½ pint whipping cream
5 tablespoons dry sherry wine
½ cup Parmesan cheese, grated

Alternate twice in individual ramekins: 1 layer of cooked broccoli and 1 layer of cooked breast of chicken or turkey. Over this pour *Hollandaise Sauce*, blended with cream, sherry and Parmesan cheese, and brown under flame. Serve piping hot.

Chicken Breasts with Ham
Serves 6

6 chicken breasts, boned, skinned and halved
6 tablespoons butter
1 large onion, minced
1 clove garlic, minced
1 tablespoon parsley, minced
½ stalk celery, minced
1 cup fresh mushrooms, sliced
1 bay leaf
Freshly ground black pepper
½ teaspoon oregano
½ teaspoon savory
1 teaspoon boveril
½ teaspoon molasses
1 cup chicken broth
½ cup dry white wine

Brown chicken in 3 tablespoons butter and transfer to a baking dish. Add remaining butter and sauté onion, garlic, parsley and celery until tender. Transfer them to the baking dish with chicken. Add the mushrooms and seasonings. Pour the chicken broth and wine over the mixture and cover tightly with foil. Bake in slow oven (325°) 1 ½ hours. Serve over a slice of cooked ham with the sauce.

Chicken Parmesan
Serves 6

SAUCE:
6 green peppers, finely chopped
4 medium onions, finely chopped
1 stalk celery, finely chopped
1 clove garlic, minced
½ cup olive oil
½ teaspoon oregano
3 bay leaves
Salt and pepper to taste
1 cup water
½ can tomato paste

Sauté vegetables in olive oil until soft. Add remaining ingredients and simmer over low heat until thick.

CHICKEN:
6 chicken breasts, skinned and boned
¼ cup butter
¼ cup Parmesan cheese, freshly grated

Place chicken breasts in baking dish, cover with sauce and bake in 350° oven 45 minutes. Remove from oven, dot with butter and sprinkle with Parmesan cheese. Bake 10 minutes longer, or until cheese is melted.

Chicken Pot Pie
Serves 6

4 chicken breasts (with skin on)

2 to 3 carrots, peeled and cut in ½-inch pieces

3 small squash, cut into ½-inch slices

2 tablespoons unsalted butter

1 medium onion

2 celery stalks

1½ cup broccoli florets

2 cups chicken broth

1 cup fresh mushrooms, sliced

8 tablespoons flour

¾ cup white wine

1 tablespoon dried tarragon

Salt and coarsely ground pepper to taste

1 egg, slightly beaten

PÂTÉ BRISÉE

1½ cups flour, sifted

½ teaspoon salt

½ cup unsalted butter

¼ cup ice water

In a pot, cover chicken breasts with water, add salt, pepper, onion and celery. Bring to a boil and simmer about 20 minutes or until chicken is tender. Remove chicken breasts from broth and cool. Reserve 1 cup of the stock containing the celery and onion. Add chicken broth to stock and bring to a boil. Add carrots, allow to cook 2 minutes, then add broccoli, cook 1 minute. Finally, add squash, allowing all vegetables to cook 1 minute together, and remove pot from burner.

Sauté mushrooms in 3 tablespoons butter, and add to other vegetables. Remove skin from cooked chicken and tear meat into 1-inch pieces. Add chicken to vegetable mixture. Blend in flour for thickening. Broth should obtain a gravy–like consistency. Add wine, tarragon, salt and pepper.

Pour chicken filling into a 2-quart buttered baking dish.

Mix the flour, salt and butter. Work butter into flour using a pastry blender or 2 knives. Mixture should look like coarse meal. Add the ice water, blending into flour mixture.

Turn dough onto floured surface, knead lightly. Wrap dough in plastic wrap and chill at least 30 minutes.

When chicken mixture is assembled, roll out dough on floured surface to a thickness of ¼ inch and place on top of dish. Trim the pastry, leaving a 1-inch border. Brush the edge of the dish with the beaten egg. Crimp edges of pastry and brush top of pastry with beaten egg. Prick holes in the top of pastry to allow steam to escape.

Bake 25 to 30 minutes in a 400° oven.

My grandson's wife, Lisa McNeir, takes time out from a busy counseling schedule to make this light and flavorful *Chicken Pot Pie.*

Chicken Breasts Minceur
Serves 4 to 6

4 breasts of chicken, halved
1 cup onions, peeled and chopped
1 cup carrots, scraped and cut into thin strips
1 cup celery, sliced
1 cup fresh mushrooms, halved
Salt and freshly ground black pepper
Basil, tarragon, parsley, marjoram and other herbs
1 cup chicken broth
1 cup white wine
1 cup cherry tomatoes
½ cup fresh or frozen green peas

OPTIONAL:
½ cup yogurt

Place vegetables in an ovenproof casserole that can be tightly covered. Season highly with freshly ground pepper and herbs. Top with chicken breasts and pour white wine over all. Cover and cook 45 minutes in oven preheated to 375°. Remove from oven and add tomatoes, mushrooms and peas. Cook 5 minutes longer and serve a chicken breast on a bed of vegetables. Part of the vegetables and liquid may be puréed in the food processor with yogurt for a delicious sauce.

When light cooking and food processors became in vogue in the late '70s, my daughter, Jean, devised this recipe for dieters.

Chicken Filling for Crêpes
Makes 14 crêpes

3 tablespoons onions, chopped
1 cup fresh mushrooms, coarsley chopped
6 tablespoons butter
½ cup flour
2 cups milk or 1 cup milk and 1 cup chicken stock
3 tablespoons chives, chopped
1 cup Swiss cheese, grated
6 tablespoons sherry
3 cups cooked chicken, diced
Salt, pepper, paprika

Make crêpes and set aside. (Or use previously frozen crêpes.) Sauté the onions and mushrooms in butter. Blend in flour. Add milk; cook and stir until mixture boils thoroughly. Add salt, pepper, paprika, chives, sherry and cheese. Lightly mix with chicken. Chill for easier handling. This mixture should be very thick. Spoon filling on crêpes and roll up. Place rolled crêpes in buttered dish. Cover with sauce that follows.

Sauce: Follow the recipe for *Chicken Filling,* except delete the chicken and increase the amount of milk to 2⅔ cups. Combine all the ingredients as directed. Pour thin sauce over crêpes and bake at 375° 15 to 20 minutes. Sprinkle with grated Parmesan cheese. Serve immediately.

Chicken and Dumplings
Serves 4 to 5

CHICKEN:
1 large fryer
1 bay leaf
1 onion, quartered
1 stalk celery
1 teaspoon of salt
½ teaspoon pepper
1 tablespoon butter
2 cups chicken broth, if needed

Remove the skin from the fryer. Boil in enough water to cover (about 2 quarts) with onion, celery, salt, pepper and butter. Remove fryer when very tender. Strain and reserve broth. Remove meat from bones. Cut meat into large pieces and return to pot with broth.

DUMPLINGS:
1 cup of buttermilk
¼ teaspoon soda
1 ½ teaspoon baking powder
½ teaspoon salt
1 egg, well beaten
1 ¼ to 1 ½ cups all–purpose flour

To make the dumplings, combine the buttermilk with soda and baking power in a small mixing bowl; stir until the mixture foams. Add salt and egg; stir in enough flour to make thick. Drop by teaspoonful on top of simmering broth; cover and simmer 15 minutes or until done. You can make a little firmer dough and roll it out to make uniform inch-square dumplings. Serve hot, adding chicken broth, if needed.

Chicken Spaghetti
Serves 8 to 10

1 large chicken
3 medium onions, chopped
1 clove garlic
1 large green pepper, chopped
1 quart chicken broth
1 #2 can tomatoes
½ pound chili brick
2 packages vermicelli
1 pound fresh mushrooms, sliced
1 pound Gruyére cheese, grated
6 eggs, beaten

Boil the chicken until tender. Debone the chicken and cut in bite-sized pieces. Sauté onions, garlic and green pepper in small amount of chicken broth. Add remaining chicken broth, the tomatoes, the chili and the liquid. Simmer 30 minutes. Cook 2 packages of vermicelli in boiling water with a little butter or olive oil. Rinse and drain well. Lightly grease a large casserole and place in it a layer of vermicelli, a layer of grated cheese, a layer of chicken pieces, the chili mixture, a layer of mushrooms, and end with a cover of grated cheese. Beat 6 eggs and pour over the top. Bake at 300° about 30 minutes or until firm.

This chicken spaghetti recipe is great for a crowd. It can be assembed a day ahead and run in the oven.

Chicken Cacciatore and Noodles
Serves 4 to 6

3 pounds chicken, cut up
½ olive oil
½ cup butter
2 onions, finely chopped
1 large green pepper, chopped
2 large cloves garlic, mashed
½ teaspoon basil
1 cup canned tomatoes
¼ cup red wine
Salt and freshly ground pepper
8 ounces noodles, boiled and
  drained

Sauté the chicken in combined olive oil and butter until golden brown. Add the onion, green pepper, garlic, salt and pepper, and simmer 5 minutes. Add basil and tomatoes. Cover and let simmer 20 minutes. Add wine and simmer 10 minutes. Serve over hot buttered noodles.

Breast of Chicken Kiev
Serves 8

¼ pound butter
1 teaspoon chopped chives or
  parsley
8 chicken breasts, boned, skinned
  and halved
¼ cup flour
2 large eggs
½ cup bread crumbs
1 cup light cooking oil

Soften butter, blending in chopped chives or parsley. Shape butter into 8 rolls about 2⅓ inches long. Chill until firm. Pound breasts to flatten. Place a butter roll on each breast, and fold meat over it to cover the butter completely. Chill thoroughly. Flour breasts, then dip first in lightly beaten egg, then in fine dry bread crumbs. Chill 1 hour. In a heavy skillet heat about 3 inches of vegetable oil to 375°. Fry chicken rolls in the oil exactly 5 minutes. Remove and drain. Serve immediately.

An interesting variation is the addition of blue cheese or brie cheese to the butter when making the chicken rolls.

Broiled Rock Cornish Game Hens
Serves 4

2 large Rock Cornish hens
½ pound bacon
4 slices bread

Preheat oven to 350° and sprinkle the Rock Cornish hens with salt and pepper and arrange in a well buttered roasting pan. Cover each with 2 to 3 half slices of bacon. Roast 50 minutes, basting several times with juices in pan. Trim 2 slices of bread, cut into triangles and sauté in 2 tablespoons of hot butter until golden on both sides. Drain on absorbent paper. Remove hens from oven, cut in half and arrange each half on a triangle of fried bread on a hot serving platter. Keep warm.

SAUCE:
½ cup cognac
½ cup cream
1 tablespoon butter
2 scallions, finely chopped
1 cup white seedless grapes
½ cup port wine
1 teaspoon lemon juice
Salt and cayenne pepper to taste
Watercress

Put roasting pan over direct heat. Add cognac to liquid in pan and cook until the liquid is reduced by half. Add cream and boil until sauce is reduced to a creamy consistency. In a small saucepan, heat 1 tablespoon butter. Add scallions and sauté 2 minutes. Add white seedless grapes and ½ cup port. Heat and ignite wine. Stir until flame burns out. Strain the cream gravy from roasting pan into wine and grape sauce. Season with salt, a dash of cayenne pepper and lemon juice.

Present on a warm platter, with each half game hen resting on a toast triangle. Pour sauce over the hens and garnish, if desired, with watercress.

FISH AND SEAFOOD

Mrs. Berry's Shrimp
Serves 4 to 6

½ cup butter
½ cup olive oil
1 ½ cups green onions, chopped
2 pounds shrimp, deveined and shelled
1 ½ teaspoons salt
¼ teaspoon pepper
2 teaspoons lemon juice
3 to 5 cloves of garlic
½ cup parsley, chopped

Sauté the onion in butter until tender. Put onion and butter in mixing bowl. Add oil, shrimp, salt, pepper, lemon juice, garlic and parsley. Toss well. Place in shallow pan 1 layer thick. Broil 3 to 5 minutes on each side. Shrimp will be pink and some edges will be crispy brown. Everything can be done ahead of time, except for broiling, and kept in refrigerator well covered. Serve over hot rice.

Mrs. Berry was the wife of one of the early managers of the Red Apple. This is a simple and delicious way to serve shrimp.

Fried Shrimp Amandine
Serves 4

10 to 15 large shrimp
½ cup flour
1 large egg, beaten
½ cup almonds, sliced
1 cup cracker meal

Butterfly uncooked shrimp. Dredge shrimp in egg wash and roll in sliced almonds and cracker meal. Deep fry in vegetable or peanut oil at 375° until brown. Remove with slotted spoon and drain well on paper towels.

Shrimp Rarebit
Serves 8

8 tablespoons butter
1 onion, chopped
4 tablespoons green pepper,
  chopped
2 pounds raw shrimp, cleaned
2 tablespoons flour
1 cup milk
1 pound grated Gruyére cheese
2 teaspoons Worcestershire sauce
¼ teaspoon dry mustard
Salt and pepper to taste

Sauté onion and pepper in 4 tablespoons butter. Add shrimp and cook just until they turn pink. In separate sauce pan, melt rest of butter and add flour. Stir until smooth and add milk gradually, then add cheese, Worcestershire sauce, mustard, salt and pepper. Stir until cheese melts. Add shrimp, green pepper and onion. Heat and serve on toast.

Shrimp Rarebit makes a good winter luncheon or Sunday night supper dish.

Shrimp Aurora
Serves 4

1 pound large shrimp, peeled and
  deveined
1 large lemon
2 tablespoons olive oil
½ teaspoon salt
¼ teaspoon pepper
1 cup *Hollandaise Sauce*, warm

Peel and devein the shrimp and arrange the shrimp in a shallow au gratin dish. Sprinkle with juice, olive oil, salt and pepper. Broil 3 or 4 minutes, turn shrimp and continue to broil 3 or 4 minutes. Spoon 1 cup of warm *Hollandaise Sauce* over the shrimp and return to the broiler about 2 minutes, or until the top is lightly browned.

Noodles Italienne
Serves 8

16 ounces spinach noodles
16 ounces lump crab meat
¼ cup sweet red pepper, chopped
6 tablespooons butter
6 tablespoons flour
1 cup light cream
Beer
½ cup slices pitted black olives
1 cup grated provolone cheese

Cook noodles 5 minutes in boiling salted water with a few drops of olive oil added. Drain and rinse with hot water. Drain crab and reserve juice. Melt butter and sauté red pepper until soft. Stir in flour. Gradually stir in cream. Add enough beer to crab juice to make 2 cups. Gradually stir this liquid into cream. Cook over low heat, stirring constantly until sauce bubbles and thickens. Stir in crab, olives and pimento. Reheat and spoon sauce over noodles. Sprinkle with cheese and serve hot.

Shrimp and Scallop Brochettes
Serves 6

¼ cup sherry
½ cup soy sauce
2 tablespoons olive oil
½ teaspoon candied ginger,
  chopped fine
36 jumbo shrimp
36 small scallops
12 slices bacon

Make a sauce by combining sherry, soy sauce, olive oil and ginger. Marinate the seafood in the sauce 30 minutes, tossing occasionally. On a 10-inch metal skewer thread an end of 1 slice of very lean bacon, the narrow end of 1 shrimp, 1 scallop and the wide end of the shrimp and pull the bacon slice up around the seafood, threading it onto the skewer. Continue to thread the brochettes using 6 shrimp, 6 scallops and 2 slices of bacon for each of the 6 skewers. Arrange the brochettes with a bacon side up on the rack of the broiler pan. Brush them with melted butter, and broil them under a preheated broiler about 5 inches from the heat for 5 minutes, or until the bacon is cooked but not crisp. Turn the brochettes, baste them with melted butter, and broil them 5 to 6 minutes more, or until the seafood and bacon are cooked. Transfer the brochettes to a heated platter and serve them with *Herbed Tomatoes* and *Potatoes Dauphine.*

Brochettes may also be cooked over an outdoor grill.

Scallops Rosemary
Serves 4

12 large scallops
¼ stick butter
1 cup white wine
½ cup green pepper, finely diced
½ cup shallots, finely chopped
½ cup green onion, finely chopped
½ cup fresh mushrooms, sliced
½ cup chicken broth
½ teaspoon each thyme, rosemary,
  sweet basil, nutmeg
Dash of cayenne
½ cup heavy cream

Sauté scallops in butter and wine until soft, but firm. Remove with slotted spoon and drain scallops on paper towels in a long pan. Cover the pan with aluminum foil and let stand in warm oven (less than 200°) Using remaining butter–wine sauce in the pan, add green pepper, shallots, green onion and mushrooms. Sauté until almost tender. Add chicken broth and simmer until wine and broth have cooked down to half the original amount. Add spices, being careful with the cayenne pepper. Add heavy cream, heated (not boiled) and pour over the warm scallops just before serving.

Deviled Crab Cakes
Serves 8

2½ pounds lump crab meat
6 tablespoons butter
1 cup scallions, finely chopped
1 cup celery, finely chopped
2 teaspoons dill, finely chopped
2 tablespoons parsley, finely
   chopped
2 tablespoons Worcestershire
   sauce
1 teaspoon Tabasco sauce
Juice of 1 lemon
Salt and freshly ground pepper
½ cup heavy cream
4 cups fresh bread crumbs
5 egg yolks
3 teaspoons dry mustard
3 cups flour
2 cups milk beaten with 2 eggs in a
   deep dish
1½ sticks clarified butter
2 lemons, quartered and seeded

Place the crab meat in a large bowl and remove any shell or cartilage. Heat the butter in a heavy skillet. Add onions and celery, and sauté over moderate heat, stirring, about 5 minutes or until vegetables are soft. Cool and add to the crab meat. Add the dill, parsley, Worcestershire sauce, Tabasco sauce, lemon juice, salt and pepper, 2 tablespoons of the cream and 2 tablespoons of the bread crumbs. In a bowl whisk together the remaining cream, egg yolks and mustard until well blended and add to the crab meat. Mix very gently, cover and refrigerate 40 minutes.

Spread the remaining bread crumbs in a pie pan, then spread the flour in another pan. With the hands, shape the mixture into 16 cakes of equal size, pressing gently to make the cakes compact. Dredge them lightly in flour, dip into the milk and egg mixture and coat lightly with bread crumbs. Place cakes on a large dish, cover and refrigerate 1 hour. Heat half the butter in a large, heavy skillet, and add half the cakes. Sauté over moderate heat about 4 minutes on each side, drain on paper towels and keep warm. Repeat with remaining cakes. Serve 2 crab cakes per person with a wedge of lemon.

Crab Meat Filling for Crêpes
Makes about 12 crêpes

2 tablespoons butter
½ cup green peppers, chopped
4 tablespoons all–purpose flour
1 cup half-and-half
1 egg yolk, beaten
1 pound crab meat
1 cup sour cream
2 tablespoons grated Romano
   cheese
Salt and pepper to taste

Sauté green pepper in butter. Add flour and cream, stirring constantly, cooking until thick. Add a little of the hot mixture to the egg yolks; then stir back into the mixture in the saucepan. When quite thick add crab meat, sour cream and cheese. Season to taste and heat to serving temperature. Spoon over crêpes and roll up. Top rolled crêpes with *Hollandaise Sauce* if desired.

Deviled Crab
Serves 4

4 hard-boiled eggs
½ cup melted butter
1 tablespoon vinegar
¾ cup boiling water
1 cup coarse cracker crumbs
8 ounces lump crab meat
1 teaspoon dry mustard
1 tablespoon catsup
½ teaspoon chili power
Dash cayenne
12 tablespoons mayonnaise
¼ teaspoon Tabasco sauce
½ teaspoon salt
1 tablespoon butter
1 tablespoon Worcestershire sauce
½ cup bread crumbs

Mash egg with butter and vinegar. Pour boiling water over cracker crumbs. Remove any shell or cartilege from crabmeat. Mix all ingredients together, put into 4 buttered shells or individual ramekins, top with bread crumbs and bake 20 minutes at 400°.

Deviled Oysters on the Half Shell
Serves 2

14 oysters in shells
2 tablespoons shallots, finely
    chopped
1 tablespoon butter
2 tablespoons flour
½ teaspoon salt
⅛ teaspoon nutmeg
Dash cayenne
1 tablespoon Worcestershire sauce
½ teaspoon chopped parsley
½ teaspoon Dijon mustard
½ pound fresh mushrooms,
    chopped
1 egg yolk, slightly beaten
½ cup cracker crumbs
1 tablespoon melted butter

Remove the oysters from shells, reserving ⅓ cup liquid; wash and chop. Wash shells. Sauté shallots in butter. Blend in flour and brown. Stir in oyster liquid, salt, nutmeg, cayenne, Worcestershire sauce, parsley, mustard and mushrooms. Add oysters and cook 3 minutes, stirring constantly. Remove from heat and add egg yolk. Arrange oyster shells in 2 pie pans half filled with rock salt. Fill oyster shells and sprinkle with mixture of crumbs and melted butter. Bake about 8 to 10 minutes at 350°.

Quick Seafood Curry
Serves 4

1 tablespoon butter
¼ cup chopped onion
1½ teaspoons curry powder
1 can cream of shrimp soup
⅓ cup milk
1 cup either shrimp or lump crab
   meat

Cook the onion in the butter and add the curry power, soup and milk. Blend well and heat until it reaches the boiling point. Remove from heat and stir in the seafood. Serve over *Indian Rice* with chopped chutney.

Indian Rice

¼ cup butter
½ cup onion, finely chopped
¼ cup slivered almonds
½ cup raisins
1 cup cooked, fluffy rice
½ cup flaked coconut

Place the raisins in very hot water and allow to stand until plump. Sauté the onions and almonds in butter until onions are tender and clear. Drain the raisins. Add the raisins, almonds and onions to the rice. Cover with the flaked coconut and then with a serving of *Quick Seafood Curry*.

A quick out-of-the-pantry supper.

Lobster Chops
Serves 4

1 cup milk, hot
4 tablespoons butter
⅓ cup flour
½ onion, grated
1 tablespoon parsley, chopped
1 medium-sized lobster or 1 can
   lobster meat
¼ teaspoon salt
⅛ teaspoon pepper
1 egg, beaten
10 saltine crackers, crushed

Scald milk. Melt butter in saucepan; remove from fire, stir in flour. Cook slowly until it bubbles. Add ⅔ of the hot milk at once, the rest gradually. Let boil slowly, stirring constantly. Add onion, parsley and lobster. Cook thoroughly; add cayenne to taste. Remove from stove. Divide in heaps—about 10. Cool thoroughly and form into chop shape. Roll in beaten egg, then rolled cracker crumbs. Chill. Fry in deep fat (375°) until golden brown and drain. Serve with *Tartar Sauce*.

My sister, Mazie Fuess, was a wonderful cook, well-known to many Arkansans—especially Episcopalians. She served *Lobster Chops* to us in the 1920's.

Seafood Quiche
Serves 8

1 tablespoon butter
¼ cup minced onion
1 tablespoon Marsala wine
½ pound shrimp, shelled, deveined
   and cut into 1-inch pieces
½ pound scallops, cut into ½-inch
   pieces
2 tablespoons parsley, minced
2 tablespoons chives, chopped
Salt and pepper to taste
1 9-inch *Pâté Brisée* (partially
   cooked 8 to 10 minutes at 400°
   in quiche dish or pie plate)
1¼ cups grated Gruyére cheese
1½ cups half-and-half
4 large eggs, lightly beaten
1 large egg yolk
½ teaspoon basil
¼ teaspoon fennel seeds
Taste of cayenne

Preheat oven to 375°, melt butter in 10-inch skillet. Add onion and sauté until soft. Add wine and cook over high heat 1 to 2 minutes, until sauce is reduced to about 2 tablespoons. Add shrimp and cook over medium heat just until pink. Stir in scallops, parsley and chives and cook about 1 minute. Season with salt and pepper. Spoon seafood into the pastry shell. Sprinkle with cheese. Combine remaining ingredients and pour over cheese. Bake 35 to 40 minutes until well puffed and set in center. Allow to cool on rack about 10 minutes before serving.

Broiled Trout
Serves 4

4 trout, cleaned and patted dry
Salt and pepper to taste
3 tablespoons Dijon mustard

Sprinkle trout with salt and pepper and spread both sides with mustard. Arrange trout on a greased broiler rack and broil about 3 inches from heat for 15 minutes, turning once.

Maître d' Hôtel Butter

½ cup unsalted butter
1 tablespoon parsley, minced
Juice of 1 lemon

While fish are broiling, cream the butter, parsley and lemon. Arrange the fish on a warm serving platter and spread with the butter. Garnish with lemon wedges and serve with *Cucumber Salad*.

Baked Red Snapper with Tomato Sauce
Serves 6

1 4– to 5-pound red snapper,
   cleaned
Salt and pepper to taste
1 tablespoon butter

SAUCE:
3 slices bacon, chopped
2 large white onions, finely
   chopped
2 cans tomatoes
1 sprig parsley, chopped
1 sprig thyme, chopped, or ½
   teaspoon, dried
2 bay leaves
Salt and pepper to taste
Hard-boiled egg slices
Lemon slices

Split underside of fish and rub inside and out with salt and pepper. Place in a baking pan, spread with butter and bake about 15 minutes at 400°. Lower heat to 350° and cover with sauce.

Fry bacon in skillet. Remove bacon and fry onions in bacon fat. When onions are soft, add tomatoes. Simmer a few minutes and add parsley, thyme, bay leaves, chopped bacon, salt and pepper. Simmer until all water has cooked out of tomatoes. Add this sauce to fish in oven and bake about 45 minutes, basting several times. Serve hot with a garnish of egg and lemon.

Filet of Sole Bon Bemme
Serves 2

2 large filets of sole
½ bottle dry white wine
1 cup fresh mushrooms, sliced
1 cup whipping cream
½ cup brown sauce
½ cup fish stock

Cut filets of sole in half and roll each slice up. Put dry white wine in skillet with rolls of sole and cover with aluminum foil. Simmer about 10 minutes. Add mushrooms and cook another 5 minutes. In a small saucepan cook whipping cream until reduced to half; pour sole juice and brown sauce into cooked–down cream. Garnish with lemon slices and parsley, and serve.

Andre Simon (of Andre's in Little Rock) showed our chef the correct (Swiss!) way to prepare this dish.

VEGETABLES

Baked Stuffed Tomatoes
Serves 6

6 medium tomatoes, insides
    scooped out with spoon, leaving
    shells
1½ cups toasted bread crumbs
1 cup beef consommé
3 slices bacon, chopped
1 cup fresh mushrooms, chopped
1 onion, chopped
1 cup green pepper, chopped
2 tablespoons parsley, finely
    chopped
1 teaspoon thyme
½ teaspoon oregano
Salt and pepper to taste

Salt and pepper tomato shells, and set aside. Scald bread crumbs with hot consommé. Sauté bacon until soft and add onions, mushrooms and green pepper until soft. Add to bread crumbs and season with other ingredients. Stuff tomatoes with stuffing mixture. Dot tops with mayonnaise and paprika. Place under broiler to brown and then bake in casserole at 350° about 20 minutes.

Corn Pudding
Serves 8

¼ cup butter
¼ cup flour
1 teaspoon salt
1½ tablespoons sugar
1¾ cups milk
3 cups fresh corn, chopped
3 eggs

Melt butter in saucepan, stir in flour, salt and sugar. Cook until bubbly, add milk and cook until thick. Stir in the corn, either chopped or whole, but chopped makes a smoother pudding. Stir in the eggs that have been beaten until frothy. Pour into a well buttered casserole and bake in a hot water bath at 350° 45 minutes until firm, like baked custard.

Corn Pudding is one of our most requested recipes. It always calls for a second helping.

Potatoes Dauphine
Serves 8

2 pounds boiling potatoes (about 5 to 6 cups sliced)

1 large clove garlic, peeled and chopped very fine

2 cups milk

1 ½ cups heavy cream

½ teaspoon salt

½ teaspoon freshly ground white pepper

1 tablespoon butter

½ cup Swiss cheese, grated

Peel the potatoes, wash and dry thoroughly. Slice fairly thin with a slicer or sharp knife. Combine the potato slices with the garlic, milk, cream, salt and pepper in a large, heavy saucepan. Bring to a boil on medium heat, stirring with a wooden spoon to prevent scorching.

When the mixture has thickened a bit, butter a shallow baking dish and pour in the potato mixture. Sprinkle with cheese and place baking dish on a cookie sheet (to catch spills and allow more even transfer of heat). Bake in a preheated 400° oven about 45 minutes, until the potatoes are nicely browned and tender when pierced with the point of a paring knife. Allow the dish to rest 15 minutes before you serve it.

Mushroom Purée with Braised Celery
Serves 6 to 8

MUSHROOM PURÉE:

1 pound fresh mushrooms

2 tablespoons butter

¾ teaspoon salt

⅛ teaspoon pepper

Pinch of nutmeg

1 cup cream

Sauté mushrooms in butter over low heat 10 minutes, or until most of the moisture in the mushrooms has cooked away, stirring occasionally. Sprinkle with salt, pepper and nutmeg. Add cream and cook over low heat 20 minutes, stirring frequently. Serve hot over *Braised Celery*.

BRAISED CELERY:

2 hearts of celery

1 cup chicken stock

3 tablespoons soft butter

½ teaspoon salt

⅛ teaspoon white pepper

Remove thick outer leaves from celery hearts. Cut remaining hearts lengthwise into 4 sections each. Arrange celery in a casserole dish and add chicken stock and soft butter. Sprinkle with salt and white pepper. Bring liquid to a boil, cover and braise over low heat 45 minutes, or until tender.

French Fried Onion Rings
Serves 6 to 8

2 cups flour
2 teaspoons salt
Dash garlic salt
2 tablespoons vegetable oil
1 tablespoon lemon juice
1½ cups water
6 onions, cut into ¼-inch rings
Vegetable oil for frying

Mix all ingredients except onions and frying oil in a food processor. Dip onion rings, separately, into batter, then drop into hot deep fat (380°). Fry until light brown. Drain on paper towels.

Baked Stuffed Onions
Serves 6

6 medium white onions
½ pound fresh mushrooms, sliced
1 tablespoon pecans, finely chopped
3 tablespoons butter
Salt and pepper to taste
1 cup beef consommé
Grated Swiss or Gruyére cheese
Paprika

Peel onions and core, leaving shells about ½ inch thick. Reserve pulp. Cook cored onions in boiling water until barely tender. Chop raw onion pulp removed in coring. Sauté chopped onion, mushrooms and pecans in butter 10 minutes. Season to taste with salt and pepper. Stuff onions with mushroom mixture. Arrange onions close together in baking pan. Pour consommé around them. Bake at 300° 30 minutes. Sprinkle with grated cheese and paprika and continue to bake 30 minutes longer. Onions may be prepared 1 day ahead and refrigerated covered until time to add consommé and bake.

Sweet Potato Croquettes
Serves 6

2 cups sweet potato, peeled, cooked and puréed
6 tablespoons brown sugar, packed down
1 egg, slightly beaten
3 tablespoons butter
½ teaspoon salt
½ cup chopped pecans
Dash nutmeg
2 cups cornflake crumbs

Combine ingredients except for crumbs. If too dry, add hot milk to moisten. Shape into balls 2 inches in diameter. Roll in cornflake crumbs. Fry in vegetable oil at 390° until brown. Serve hot.

Winter's Night Casserole of Sweet Potato and Apple
Serves 6

6 medium sweet potatoes
4 large apples
Butter to dot
Nutmeg to taste
Ground cloves to taste
Cinnamon to taste
Salt to taste
1 ½ cups orange juice
Brown sugar to sprinkle (optional)

Boil sweet potatoes until firm. Do not overcook. Pare and slice apples crosswise. Arrange in casserole dish—layer of sweet potatoes, layer of apples, keeping proportions equal. Dot with butter and season to taste from spices above. Make another layer in the same way. Pour orange juice over the dish and sprinkle brown sugar on the top if desired. Cook in 350° oven until apples are tender, about 30 minutes.

Spinach Casserole
Serves 6

3 pounds fresh spinach, washed or
   2 packages frozen, chopped
   spinach
1 tablespoon butter
Dash nutmeg
Salt, pepper to taste
¼ cup heavy cream
½ pound fresh mushrooms
1 cup white bread, cubed
2 tablespoons butter

Cook, drain and run spinach through a blender. Add 1 tablespoon butter, nutmeg, salt, pepper and cream. Sauté mushrooms and cubed bread in 2 tablespoons butter until crisp and golden brown. Put spinach into ramekins and sprinkle the croutons on top. Heat through in 400° oven 10 to 15 minutes.

Fried Squash
Serves 4

3 slices bacon, chopped
1 medium onion, chopped
6 medium squash, chopped
Salt and pepper
Pinch of sugar
Fantastic Seasoning, or your
   favorite herb seasoning

Parboil squash until almost done. Sauté bacon and onions until soft. Pour off grease. Add squash to skillet and mix well. Season and serve hot.

Stuffed Squash
Serves 6

12 small yellow crooked neck squash
2 tablespoons onion, finely chopped
1 teaspoon sweet red pepper, chopped
1 teaspoon parsley, chopped
3 tablespoons bread crumbs
1 hard-boiled egg, finely chopped
2 tablespoons butter
Salt and pepper

Cook unpeeled squash in boiling salted water (or steam) just until tender. Cool, cut hole in top and dig centers out with a teaspoon, being careful not to break the squash as they are tender. Set aside the shells and chop the pulp finely. Sauté onion, parsley and red pepper in butter until onion is yellow and soft. Add squash pulp, 2 tablespoons bread crumbs and egg. Mix and season to taste with salt and pepper. Fill cavities of squash with the stuffing. Sprinkle with 1 tablespoon bread crumbs, buttered. Place on a buttered cookie sheet and bake 20 minutes at 350° or until the crumbs are brown and sizzling.

My mother-in-law cooked squash this way—and we loved it!

Squash, Broccoli or Spinach Casserole
Serves 4 to 6

2 cups cooked squash
⅔ cup sour cream
4 eggs
½ teaspoon nutmeg
1 cup crackers, crushed
White pepper
2 tablespoons grated onion
Cavender's Greek seasoning, to taste

Put all ingredients in a food processor and blend well. Pour into buttered 1-quart soufflé dish nearly to top. Bake in 350° oven and cook about 30 minutes or until firm, like baked custard, and brown on top.

You may use broccoli or spinach in place of squash. ⅓ cup of mayonnaise added to broccoli is a good touch.

Baked Zucchini Squash
Serves 8

6 medium-sized zucchini
1 small onion, minced
2 tablespoons butter
3 cups soft bread crumbs
½ cup grated Parmesan cheese
3 tablespoons minced parsley
1 teaspoon salt
⅛ teaspoon pepper
2 beaten eggs
¼ cup sour cream
½ teaspoon Beau Monde
  seasoning
¼ teaspoon thyme
Buttered bread crumbs

Cook cubed squash in very little water, about ¼ cup, 3 to 5 minutes until tender, and drain. Sauté onion in butter. Mash squash, combine with crumbs, cheese, onion, butter, parsley, salt, pepper, eggs, sour cream, Beau Monde and thyme. Place in greased 6-cup casserole, sprinkle with buttered bread crumbs and a little more cheese. Bake at 350° about 30 minutes.

Green Bean and Mushroom Casserole
Serves 8 to 10

1 pound fresh mushrooms
½ cup butter
¼ cup flour
2 cups milk
1 cup light cream
¾ cup sharp Cheddar cheese
2 teaspoons soy sauce
1 teaspoon salt
2 pounds fresh stringed green
  beans
1 can water chestnuts
¾ cup toasted slivered almonds

Sauté mushrooms in butter. Add flour and cook until smooth. Add to this milk and cream and keep stirring. Add cheese and seasonings. Meanwhile cook stringed green beans until barely tender and drain. Mix beans with mushroom cheese sauce and water chestnuts. Pour into casserole and sprinkle with almonds. Bake 20 minutes in 375° oven until it bubbles through the top and is very hot.

Stuffed Eggplant with Crab Meat
Serves 6

1 medium eggplant
½ cup bread crumbs
1 tablespoon butter
2 tablespoons Parmesan cheese,
   freshly grated
4 tablespoons butter
2 large scallions, chopped
2 tablespoons parsley, chopped
½ pound lump crab meat
¼ teaspoon salt
¼ teaspoon pepper

Boil whole eggplant in water 20 minutes. Drain and when cool enough to handle, cut lengthwise and carefully remove pulp, leaving a shell ¼ inch thick. Chop the pulp and reserve. Arrange the shells in a shallow baking dish. Preheat oven to 400°.

Brown bread crumbs in butter and mix with Parmesan cheese. Sauté scallions and parsley in butter. Add crab meat. Add eggplant pulp and sprinkle with salt and pepper.

Pile stuffing into eggplant shells. Sprinkle with the bread crumb--cheese mixture and dot each portion with butter. Bake in hot oven (375°) 20 minutes and serve hot.

Scalloped Eggplant or Squash
Serves 6

1 large eggplant or
   2 medium squash
1 small onion, chopped
3 stalks celery, chopped
½ cup butter
2 hard boiled eggs, chopped
1 cup bread crumbs
Salt and pepper
1 cup milk
2 eggs, well beaten
¼ cup mayonnaise

Steam eggplant or squash, drain and mash. Sauté onion and celery in butter, add to eggplant. Mix remaining ingredients and place in buttered casserole. Cover with bread crumbs and bake 45 minutes in moderate oven (350°).

Succotash
Serves 8

4 tablespoons butter
¼ cup onion, chopped
1 garlic bud, minced
4 ears sweet corn, cut off the cob
6 medium tomatoes, peeled and
    quartered
1 pound fresh butterbeans
½ pound okra, sliced
1 cup chicken broth
¼ cup half-and-half
Pinch of sugar
Salt and pepper to taste

Sauté onions, garlic and corn in butter in heavy skillet until just tender. Add butter beans, tomatoes, okra and chicken broth. Cover skillet and simmer about 20 minutes until vegetables are done and liquid has cooked down. Add just enough cream to moisten the succotash.

This is a favorite Southern dish in the summertime when all the vegetables are fresh from the garden.

SOUFFLÉS

Herbert Thomas loved soufflés and encouraged me to include them on the menu at the Red Apple, even though they are usually considered too delicate to serve on a mass production basis. We thought they would add an elegant touch to the dinners and decided to serve a cheese or vegetable soufflé with every dinner. Several dessert soufflés are also on the menu.

I was lucky enough to find a woman who loved learning to cook new dishes, Winsell Harris. She was a good student and has been turning out beautiful soufflés for nineteen years. Recently she told me she attributes part of her success to the copper bowl Herbert gave her during her first year on the job. She said he told her that "egg whites would be lighter if I beat them in a copper bowl." She is still using the techniques she and I worked out in the beginning—and she has no problem with falling soufflés! She says, after years of cooking the same recipes, that "every day is a new challenge." She enjoys the appreciation the guests show for her effort.

Winsell has some pointers to share with novice soufflé chefs:

1. Preheat the oven and make sure the temperature is accurate.
2. If you have the stamina, whip egg whites by hand for the lightest soufflé possible.
3. Use the warm water bath during cooking because it will prolong the soufflé's puffiness during serving.
4. Practice and a good recipe will assure success.

Soufflés are really comparatively easy to make, once the basics are learned, and the variations are endless. The components of a soufflé are a sauce about as thick as a thick syrup (including melted butter, flour, milk and egg yolks) and the beaten egg whites. The sauce may include grated cheese, chopped vegetables, seafood and any kind of flavoring and seasoning. The egg whites should be beaten until not quite stiff and carefully folded into the sauce.

We think that you'll find the tried-and-true recipes to be a delight to your family and guests, and we do recommend the copper bowl.

Soufflés are traditionally served as a side dish with dinner at the Inn, but can become a no–fuss main dish when combined with a green salad, French bread, wine and fresh fruit.

Soufflés are standard fare at the Red Apple. A soufflé is served by the waiter on a silver tray with every dinner at night as a side dish.

Broccoli Soufflé
Serves 4

10 ounces fresh broccoli, washed
   and trimmed
3 tablespoons butter
3 tablespoons flour
1 teaspoon salt
1 cup milk
⅛ teaspoon nutmeg
Cayenne pepper to taste
1 teaspoon lemon juice
4 eggs, separated

OPTIONAL TOPPING:
¼ cup sour cream
¼ cup mayonnaise
Dash curry powder

Preheat oven to 350°. Steam broccoli just until tender. Drain and chop fine or put through a food processor. Melt butter. Add flour and salt, cooking and stirring until bubbly. Add milk. Cook and stir until thick. Add nutmeg, cayenne, lemon juice and broccoli. Cool slightly and add beaten egg yolks. Beat egg whites until stiff. When the broccoli mixture is cool, fold egg whites into it. Pour into a buttered 6-cup souffle dish, place in a hot water bath in oven 40 to 50 minutes or until firm. Serve plain or with a sour cream–mayonnaise sauce to which a dash of curry powder has been added.

The flavor may be varied by adding 1 teaspoon dried dill weed.

Eggplant Soufflé
Serves 6 to 8

1 medium-sized eggplant
2 tablespoons butter
2 tablespoons flour
1 cup milk
1 cup grated cheddar or Gruyére
   cheese
¾ cup soft bread crumbs
2 teaspoons grated onion
1 tablespoon tomato catsup
Salt, pepper, cayenne
2 eggs
Broiled bacon, chopped, for
   garnish

Peel eggplant, cut into small pieces and cook in boiling, salted water until tender. Drain thoroughly and mash. Make a cream sauce with the butter, flour and milk. When thickened and smooth, add the mashed eggplant, cheese, crumbs, onion, catsup and seasoning to taste; add well beaten egg yolks. Fold in stiffly beaten egg whites, pour into a buttered 8-cup soufflé dish and bake in a 350° oven about 45 minutes. Garnish with broiled bacon and serve immediately.

Sliced, fresh mushrooms, sautéed, could be added along with the eggplant. Or for a main dish, shrimp would be a nice addition.

Original Cheese Soufflé
Serves 6

3 tablespoons butter
¼ cup flour
1⅞ cup milk
1 teaspoon salt
Dash cayenne pepper
1 teaspoon prepared mustard
2 drops Worcestershire sauce
1 cup grated cheddar or American
   cheese, packed
6 eggs, separated

Make a cream sauce by melting the butter and blending in the flour. Cook until bubbly. Add the milk, salt, cayenne, mustard and Worcestershire sauce, and bring to a boil, stirring constantly. Boil 1 minute (time it!). Remove from heat and cool slightly. Add the cheese. Beat the egg yolks until thick and add the cheese mixture, stirring constantly. Beat the egg whites until stiff. Fold into the cheese mixture carefully; pour into a buttered 6-cup soufflé dish. Bake at 300° in a hot water bath for 2 hours, or until a silver knife inserted into the center comes out clean.

This soufflé keeps a day in the icebox after baking, so it can be a leftover successfully.

Vegetable Soufflé
Serves 8

¼ cup butter
½ cup flour
1 teaspoon salt
1 tablespoon sugar
1¾ cups milk
3 cups vegetables, cooked and
   finely chopped
Dash of cayenne pepper
¼ teaspoon nutmeg
⅛ teaspoon thyme
Dash garlic salt
3 eggs, separated

Melt butter in a saucepan, stir in flour, salt and sugar. Add milk and cook until thick and smooth. Stir in the 3 cups of cooked vegetables (anything except tomatoes and beets) or any one vegetable like squash, corn, or broccoli. Add well beaten egg yolks. Add rest of seasonings and correct seasonings to taste (you might consider adding a fresh herb or some black pepper). Beat egg whites until stiff and fold into the vegetable mixture. Pour into buttered 2-quart soufflé dish and bake in a hot water bath about 45 minutes at 350°.

A great way to use up leftover vegetables in various combinations.

Squash Soufflé
Serves 4

2 pounds squash
1½ tablespoons butter
½ teaspoon onion juice, optional
½ teaspoon Worcestershire sauce
1 tablespoon flour
Salt and pepper to taste
2 eggs, separated

Steam or boil squash until just tender. Drain and chop. Melt butter in skillet, add onion juice (or chopped onion), Worcestershire sauce, blending in flour and seasonings. Add squash and remove from heat. Beat egg yolks, add to squash, mixing well. Fold in stiffly beaten egg whites and put in casserole dish. Cook in 350° oven 35 to 45 minutes.

Three Cheese Soufflé
Serves 6

¼ cup unsalted butter
⅓ cup flour
1¾ cup milk
½ teaspoon salt
¼ teaspoon freshly ground black pepper
½ teaspoon freshly ground nutmeg
Dash cayenne pepper
½ teaspoon dry mustard
6 eggs, separated
1 egg white
¾ cup grated Gruyére cheese
¼ cup grated Gorganzola cheese
¼ cup grated Parmesan cheese

Heat oven to 400°. Use 2 tablespoons butter to butter a 2-quart soufflé dish or 6 individual ramekins. In a saucepan melt the remaining butter over moderate heat. Add flour and cook, stirring 3 or 4 minutes without allowing mixture to color. Scald milk in another saucepan over moderately high heat. Gradually whisk the hot milk into the roux. Bring to boil, while stirring constantly with whisk. Cook about 2 minutes until the bechemel thickens. Add salt, pepper, cayenne, nutmeg and mustard. Remove from heat. One at a time beat the egg yolks into the bechemel sauce. Stir in the 3 cheeses. Beat the egg whites until stiff but not dry or grainy. Stir about ¼ of the beaten whites into the sauce. Fold the remaining egg whites into the soufflé base. Turn the mixture into the soufflé dish or ramekins. Bake in lower third of oven about 35 minutes. If using individual ramekins, bake 20 to 25 minutes. Sprinkle remaining Parmesan over top. Bake about 5 minutes longer until cheese is melted. Serve immediately.

SAUCES

Basting Sauce for Broiling Chickens

2 cloves garlic, crushed
¾ cup olive oil
Juice of 2 lemons
1 tablespoon Worcestershire sauce
1 teaspoon salt
½ teaspoon ground pepper

Combine all ingredients in food processor or saucepan. Baste chickens before broiling.

Marinade for Shish Kebobs or Lamb Chops

1 cup salad oil
½ cup red wine vinegar
1 large jar Dijon mustard
2 tablespoons Worcestershire
  sauce
2 teaspoons salt
2 teaspoons curry powder
1 tablespoon black pepper
2 teaspoons dried marjoram
2½ cloves garlic, peeled and
  crushed
1 large onion, peeled and grated
2 stalks celery, grated

Blend ingredients and let stand overnight. Marinate meat 3 or 4 hours before cooking.

Raisin Sauce

1 cup sugar
½ cup water
1 cup seedless white raisins
1 cup oranges, finely chopped with rind left on
2 tablespoons butter
2 tablespoons vinegar
⅛ tablespoon Worcestershire sauce
½ teaspoon salt
¼ teaspoon ground cloves
⅛ teaspoon ground mace
1 cup currant jelly
¼ cup ham drippings (if you have them)
2 teaspoons cornstarch

Mix together all the ingredients (except ham drippings and cornstarch) and bring to a boil. Cook until raisins are plump. Add drippings and cornstarch dissolved in a little cold water. Cook until clear.

Sauce for ham should be light bodied and thin. This is a good sauce to keep in your refrigerator. Use it on ham, corned beef or smoked tongue. It is especially nice to dress up leftover ham made into timbales or loaves.

Rémoulade Sauce
Makes 1½ cups

1 cup *Vinaigrette Dressing*
2 tablespoons tomato ketchup
4 tablespoons Louisiana mustard
2 scallions, chopped
¼ cup celery, finely chopped

Combine ingredients. When serving with shrimp, let the shrimp stand in the sauce overnight. The Louisiana mustard has horseradish which gives it the zip.

French Sour Cream Sauce

½ cup sour cream
3 tablespoons *Vinaigrette Dressing*
1 tablespoon grated horseradish
Pepper to taste

Combine ingredients; mix well.

Good on green beans, broccoli or spinach.

Sauce for Spanish Omelet
Serves 8

3 tablespoons olive oil
1 cup onion, chopped
½ cup green pepper, chopped
½ cup red pepper, chopped
½ cup celery
6 medium tomatoes, peeled and
　chopped
1 small can tomato purée
½ pound fresh mushrooms, sliced
Salt and pepper to taste
1 ½ tablespoon chili powder
¼ teaspoon celery salt
⅛ teaspoon oregano
⅛ teaspoon sugar
¼ teaspoon thyme
Sprinkling of chives

Sauté onions, peppers and celery in olive oil until barely tender. Add tomatoes and purée diluted with a can of water. Add mushrooms and seasonings and simmer slowly until slightly thick.

Spanish Omelet is a good, quick supper dish. This sauce is versatile and can be kept frozen for lots of uses.

Hollandaise Sauce
4 servings

¼ pound butter
3 egg yolks
2 tablespoons lemon juice
¼ teaspoon salt
Pinch cayenne pepper

Melt butter in saucepan until it is bubbling, but not brown. Place other ingredients in an electric blender or food processor. Cover container and turn motor quickly on and off at high speed. Remove cover, add hot butter in a steady stream. When all butter is added, turn motor off. Serve immediately or keep warm by setting container into a saucepan containing 2 inches hot water.

Basic Tomato Sauce

1 large clove of garlic, peeled
2 tablespoons olive oil
3 cups ripe tomatoes, peeled and
　chopped
1 teaspoon salt
1 tablespoon dried basil

Combine the garlic and olive oil in a deep skillet. Simmer over very low heat until the garlic has browned lightly. Add the tomatoes, salt, pepper and basil. Cook over a low heat, stirring frequently, until the sauce is well mixed and starts to boil. Turn heat very low and cook until the juices have evaporated (about 4 to 5 minutes) and the sauce thickens sufficiently so that a spoon pulled through it leaves a light path. Taste for seasoning.

Rum Cake

Serves 10

1 package yellow cake mix
1 package vanilla instant pudding
  mix
4 eggs
½ cup vegetable oil
½ cup water
½ cup Bacardi rum
½ cup pecans, chopped

Beat together cake mix, pudding mix, eggs, vegetable oil, water and rum. Sprinkle ¼ cup chopped nuts in 10-inch greased and floured bundt or tube pan. Pour in batter, sprinkle ¼ cup nuts on top and bake 1 hour at 350°. Invert on cake rack to cool.

RUM SAUCE:
1 cup sugar
¼ pound butter or margarine
¼ cup water

Bring these ingredients to a boil 1 minute. Add 2 ounces or ¼ cup of rum. Pour half of sauce over cake while still in pan. Invert and remove cake from pan. Pour remaining sauce over the other side.

I don't ordinarily recommend a cake mix, but this one is superb.

Pecan Meringues

2 egg whites, stiffly beaten
¼ teaspoon salt
1 box light brown sugar
1 teaspoon soda
1 quart pecan halves

Add salt to beaten egg whites. Sift brown sugar in a separate bowl and sprinkle in the soda, mixing well. Fold sugar into the egg whites. Add pecans, a few at a time, until well coated. Using a teaspoon, drop mixture in small mounds on a greased cookie sheet. (Mixture will fill several cookie sheets.) Bake about 30 minutes in a moderate oven (350°). Remove with spatula and cool.

Chocolate Angel Food Cake
Serves 8 to 10

1 ½ cup egg whites at room temperature
1 ¼ teaspoon cream of tartar
½ teaspoon salt
1 ¾ cup granulated sugar
1 teaspoon vanilla
¼ teaspoon almond flavoring
¾ cup plus 2 tablespoons cake flour
¼ cup cocoa

Beat egg whites with wire whisk. Add cream of tartar and salt when eggs are frothy. Continue beating until a point of egg whites will stand upright. Gradually beat in sugar which has been sifted twice. Fold in the flavoring. Fold in the flour which has been sifted 3 times with sugar and cocoa. Pour into dry ungreased angel food cake pan and bake at 325° about 65 minutes. When done, remove from oven and invert cake pan until cake is entirely cold. Cover with the frosting.

CHOCOLATE ANGEL FOOD CAKE FROSTING:
1 cup whipping cream
1 cup powdered sugar, sifted
3 tablespoons cocoa

Mix together and cool in refrigerator 1 hour. Whip until stiff enough to ice outside of cake.

Orange Crêpes
Serves 6 to 9

3 eggs
2 egg yolks
½ cup milk
½ cup orange juice
2 tablespoons salad oil
1 cup all–purpose flour, sifted
¾ teaspoon salt
1 tablespoon sugar
1 tablespoon orange rind, grated

Beat eggs and egg yolks. Add remaining ingredients and beat until smooth. Let stand at room temperature at least 1 hour. Lightly brush hot 7-inch or 8-inch skillet with salad oil. Add 2 tablespoons batter to skillet; turn and tip skillet so mixture covers bottom evenly. Batter will set immediately into thin lacy pancake. When it browns in about 15 or 20 seconds, loosen with spatula and flip over. Brown other side in just a few seconds and turn crêpe out onto foil or plastic wrap. Repeat with remaining batter to make 18 crêpes.

ORANGE SAUCE:
½ cup butter, softened
½ cup confectioners sugar
1 tablespoon orange rind, grated
3 tablespoons orange liqueur
⅓ cup orange juice
1 cup orange sections, optional

Cream butter with sugar and orange rind. Gradually blend in orange liqueur. Spread about ½ teaspoon of mixture over side of crêpe that was browned second. Roll up crêpes with orange mixture and place with the orange juice in blazer or crêpe pan directly over flame. Heat until bubbly. Add orange sections and heat 2 or 3 minutes longer. Makes about 18 crêpes.

Shipp's Special
Serves 6

6 eggs, separated
1½ cups sugar
¾ cup cream of wheat (raw)
1 cup pecans, finely ground
1 teaspoon vanilla
Pinch salt
1 pint heavy cream, whipped

Blend egg yolks and sugar until smooth. Add cream of wheat, pecans, vanilla and salt. Mix well. Beat egg whites until stiff and fold into cake mixture. Pour into 2 greased round cake pans, or 1 rectangular pan (9×13 inches). Bake 30 minutes at 350°. Let cool before removing from pan. If baked in rectangular pan, cut in two to make 2 layers. Ice each layer with whipping cream, stack and ice overall.

I had this delicious dessert at a friend's house, and asked for the recipe. She was gracious enough to share it with me for the cookbook. It was a specialty of her mother, Mrs. A.C. Shipp.

Russian Black Cherries
Serves 4

1 #2 can black cherries
2 tablespoons rum or whiskey
1 small glass currant jelly
½ cup sour cream

Pit and drain cherries. Beat jelly and rum together. Add cherries. Refrigerate until chilled. Serve topped with sour cream.

Cookie Gun Dough

1 pound butter
1½ cups sugar
1 whole egg and yolk of another
2 teaspoons vanilla
5 cups flour

Cream butter and sugar by hand or in bowl of food processor. Add eggs and mix. Add vanilla and then flour and mix well. Chill at least 30 minutes and fill the cookie gun and make into desired shapes. Bake on greased cookie sheet in 350° oven about 10 minutes or until light brown.

Plum Pudding
Serves 8 to 10

2 cups suet, chopped
1 cup apple, chopped
2 cups seedless raisins
1 cup currants
1 cup light molasses
1 cup cold water
3 cups flour
½ teaspoon salt
1 teaspoon soda
2 teaspoons cinnamon
½ teaspoon cloves
½ teaspoon allspice

Combine suet, fruits, molasses and water. Add sifted dry ingredients and mix thoroughly. Fill greased molds ⅔ full; cover tightly and steam 3 hours on rack in covered container, using small amount of boiling water. Serve hot with *Hard Sauce* or *Mocha Sauce.*

HARD SAUCE:
⅓ cup butter, softened
1 cup confectioners sugar or ¾ cup granulated sugar
⅔ teaspoon vanilla, brandy or other flavoring

Cream butter thoroughly and beat in sugar gradually, continuing until smooth and fluffy. Add flavoring drop by drop to keep from separating. For a richer sauce, beat in ¼ cup heavy cream (lukewarm). Chill.

Mocha Sauce: Make *Hard Sauce* with cream and flavor with 2 tablespoons strong coffee and 2 teaspoons dry cocoa.

Boccone Dolce
(Sweet Mouthful)
Serves 8

MERINGUE LAYERS:
4 egg whites
Pinch of salt
¼ teaspoon cream of tartar
1 cup sugar

Preheat oven to very slow 250°. Beat egg whites with salt and cream of tartar until stiff. Gradually beat in sugar and continue to beat until meringue is stiff and glossy. Line baking sheets with waxed paper and on the paper trace 3 circles, each 8 inches in diameter. Spread the meringue evenly over the circles, about ¼ inch thick and bake in slow oven 20 to 25 minutes, or until meringue is pale gold but still pliable. Remove from oven and carefully peel waxed paper from bottom. Place on cake racks to dry.

FILLING:

**6 ounces semi-sweet chocolate
  pieces**

3 tablespoons water

3 cups heavy cream

⅓ cup sugar

1 pint fresh strawberries

Melt chocolate and water in a double boiler over hot water. Whip cream until stiff, gradually add sugar and beat until very stiff. Clean and slice strawberries.

Place a meringue layer on serving plate and spread with a thin coating of melted chocolate. Then spread a layer of the whipped cream on top and cover with a layer of the strawberries. Put a second layer of meringue on top and repeat. Top with third layer of meringue and frost sides smoothly with remaining whipped cream. Top may be decorated with melted chocolate squeezed through a pastry tube in a random pattern or with whole ripe strawberries. Refrigerate 2 hours before serving.

Meringues, strawberries and chocolate are an irresistible combination. This Italian recipe combines all three and is as delicious as it looks.

Silk Pie
Serves 6

½ cup butter, softened

¾ cup sugar

4 tablespoons butter, melted

1 tablespoon cocoa

1 teaspoon vanilla

2 eggs at room temperature

¾ cup chopped pecans

¼ teaspoon vanilla

1 pint heavy cream, whipped

Cream butter and sugar. Combine melted butter and cocoa. Blend chocolate mixture into sugar mixture and add vanilla. Add 2 eggs, one at a time, beating for 5 minutes after each addition. (Having eggs at room temperature will make the mixture much smoother.) Pour into baked pie shell; spread chopped pecans over top and cover with cream whipped with sugar to taste and vanilla. Refrigerate 6 hours before serving.

Bavarian Cream Pie
Serves 6 to 8

1½ envelopes plain gelatin
¼ cup cold water
1 tablespoon hot water
3 eggs, separated
½ cup sugar
½ cup milk
½ teaspoon vanilla
Whipped cream
1 square semi-sweet chocolate,
  grated

Soften gelatin in cold water and add hot water to dissolve. Beat egg yolks slightly and mix with sugar. Add milk and gelatin to egg mixture and cook in double boiler stirring until thick. Add vanilla and cool. Beat egg whites until stiff and gradually add ½ cup sugar. Fold into cooled mixture and pour into a baked 9-inch pie shell. Cover top with whipped cream and grate chocolate on top.

This pie was served at the old Sam Peck Hotel in Little Rock and before that at the Washington Hotel in Fayetteville.

Orange Soufflé
Serves 4

8 eggs, separated
2 cups sugar
½ teaspoon salt
Juice of 4 medium-sized oranges
Grated rind of 4 oranges

Beat egg yolks until thick and lemon colored. Gradually add sugar and salt and continue beating. Add the orange juice and rind. Beat egg whites until stiff and fold into mixture. Turn batter into a generously buttered soufflé dish and set the dish in a pan of hot, not boiling, water. Bake soufflé 1 hour at 350° or until firm. Serve hot topped with *Crème Fresche*.

Herbert brought this recipe for *Orange Soufflé* back from Spain. It was a favorite.

Chocolate Crème Fresche

½ pint whipping cream
4 tablespoons cocoa
3 ounces cream cheese, softened
½ teaspoon almond extract
¾ cup powdered sugar, sifted

Whip cream and fold in cocoa. Blend cream cheese and almond extract in mixer or food processor. Add whipped cream and cocoa and blend briefly, then add powdered sugar and blend briefly. Can be served with chocolate soufflé or on any chocolate dessert.

Soufflé Grand Marnier
Serves 2

1 ½ tablespoons butter
¾ tablespoon orange rind, grated
5 ounces milk
3 egg yolks
¼ cup cornstarch
1 ½ tablespoons Grand Marnier
¼ cup sugar
4 egg whites
Pinch salt
Pinch cream of tartar
2 tablespoons sugar

Place rack in middle of oven and preheat oven to 400°. Butter well the sides and bottom of two 12-ounce soufflé bowls. Sprinkle them with sugar, dumping out the excess. Measure and mix together the cornstarch, sugar and salt. Place the butter and milk in heavy saucepan and while still cold, stir in the dry ingredients and the grated orange rind. Cook the mixture over medium heat, stirring constantly with a wire whip until the mixture thickens. Remove from heat and thoroughly stir in the egg yolks and the Grand Marnier. Beat the egg whites with the cream of tartar until limp; add the sugar and continue beating at high speed to develop a good meringue. Take half the beaten egg whites and using a rubber spatula stir them into the sauce to lighten it. Give the remaining egg whites several good whips and then fold them into the lightened sauce. Do not overfold as you will deflate the mixture. Divide the mixture between the prepared bowls. (At this point, you may delay baking the soufflés up to 30 minutes). Place the soufflés in the preheated oven and cook 15 minutes. Serve with *St. Cecilia Sauce*.

ST. CECILIA SAUCE:
2 egg yolks
Pinch of salt
¾ cup powdered sugar
1 cup whipping cream
2 tablespoons Grand Marnier

Beat the yolks until pale yellow. Add salt and powdered sugar. Whip the cream and fold into the egg yolk mixture with the Grand Marnier. Refrigerate until ready to use.

Jacque & Suzanne's Restaurant used to serve this sauce.

Index

Angel Biscuits, 40
Appetizers
    Blini, 116
    Caviar Mousse, 99
    Cheese Ball with Pecans, 97
    Cheese Straws, 126
    Chicken Liver Pâté, 120
    Guacamole Dip, 143
    Hot Cheese Balls, 142
    Hot Crab Meat Dip, 97
    Marinated Tomatoes, 98
    Mushrooms Stuffed with Escargots, 142
    Mushrooms Stuffed with Oysters, 141
    Mushrooms Stuffed with Spinach, 99
    Oysters Broiled in Bacon, 96
    Quick Asparagus Dip, 143
    Roquefort Wafers, 141
    Salted Pecans with Rosemary, 96
    Shrimp and Cheese Ball, 135
    Sliced Beef Tenderloin, 97
    Smoked Oyster Dip, 98
    Smoked Salmon Mousse, 142
    Tomato Croustades, 143
Apple(s)
    Cake with Hot Buttered Rum Sauce, 59
    Crisp, 71
    Dutch Apple Bread, 145
    Red Apple Apple Pie, 84
    Winter's Night Casserole of Sweet Potato and, 193
Apricot, Dreamy Salad, 163
Apricots or Green Gage Plum Salad, 164
Argolemono Soup, 154
Artichoke(s)
    and Shrimp Casserole, 53
    Bottoms with Green Peas, 112
    Crab Salad, 157
Asparagus
    Deviled Eggs with, 137
    Dip, Quick, 143
    Salad Mold, 89
    Vinaigrette, 46
Avocado(s)
    and Grapefruit Salad, 129
    Guacamole Dip, 143
    Mousse for Luncheon, 157
    Soup, Cold Cucumber or, 50
    with Lobster Salad, 158
Baby New Potatoes and Peas, 115
Bacon
    Crisp, 36
    Oysters Broiled in, 96
    Spoon Bread, 144
Banana Bran Muffins, 41

Baked
    Ham Eden Isle, 172
    Red Snapper with Tomato Sauce, 189
    Stuffed Onions, 192
    Stuffed Tomatoes, 190
    Zucchini Squash, 195
Barley
    Soup, 152
    Steamed, 89
Basic Tomato Sauce, 204
Basting Sauce for Broiling Chickens, 202
Bavarian Cream Pie, 210
Béarnaise Sauce, 111
Beef
    Brisket with Kraut, 91
    Burgundy, 170
    Cannelloni, 168
    Chateaubriand with Sauce Béarnaise, 110
    Deviled Rib Bones, 73
    Filet Mignon with Sauce Bordelaise, 167
    Homemade Chili, 59
    Mushroom-Filled Meat Loaf, 92
    Reuben Sandwich, 67
    Roast Prime Rib of, 101
    Tenderloin, Sliced, 97
    Tournedos of, 167
    Vegetable Soup, 60
    Wellington, 105
    William O. Douglas' Wood-Smoke Steak, 77
Beet Salad, Molded, 119
Beverages
    Iced Danish Mary, 126
    May Wine, 114
    Wassail, 133
Black-Eyed Peas with Green Tomato Pickle, 69
Blender Crepes, 150
Boccone Dolce, 208
Bordelaise Sauce, 167
Boston Lettuce Salad with Walnut Dressing, 103
Braised
    Celery, Mushroom Purée with, 191
    Lamb Shanks, 88
Breads
    Angel Biscuits, 40
    Bacon Spoon Bread, 144
    Banana Bran Muffins, 41
    Bread Pudding with Orange Sauce, 90
    Buckwheat Blini, 116
    Buttered and Toasted Rolls, 52
    Buttermilk Biscuits, 147
    Buttermilk Pancakes, 146
    Coffee Cake, 38
    Corn Sticks, 48

Cracker Balls, 60
Croutons, 113
Date and Nut Bread, 146
Dutch Apple Bread, 145
Hot Crackers, 101
Hush Puppies, 76
Irish Soda Bread, 54
Jean's Famous Rolls, 83
Lemon Muffins, 46
Mexican Corn Bread, 145
Orange Nut Bread, 146
Pecan Waffles, 147
Pone Bread, 71
Popovers, 37
Prune Sour Cream Coffee Cake, 43
Skillet Corn Bread, 61
Sourdough Biscuits, 131
Spoon Bread, 102
Twelve-Minute Cheese Biscuits, 144
Bread Pudding with Orange Sauce, 90
Breast of Chicken Kiev, 180
Broccoli
    Casserole, 194
    Ring, 109
    Soufflé, 199
Broiled
    Rock Cornish Game Hens, 181
    Trout with Cucumber Salad, 188
Brownie Pie, 61
Brussels Sprouts in Consommé, 129
Buckwheat Blini, 116
Buttered and Toasted Rolls, 52
Buttermilk
    Biscuits, 147
    Pancakes, 146
    Pound Cake, 65
Cabbage Slaw, 76
Caesar Salad, 82
Cake(s)
    Apple with Hot Buttered Rum Sauce, 59
    Buttermilk Pound, 65
    Carrot, 74
    Charlotte Russe, 121
    Chocolate Angel Food, 206
    Chocolate Fudge Cup, 137
    Chocolate Roll, 94
    Coconut, 54
    Coffee, 38
    Deviled Crab, 185
    Jam with Caramel Icing, 65
    Lemon Christmas, 133
    Potato, 42
    Prune Sour Cream Coffee, 43

    Rum, 205
    Sour Cream Chocolate, 64
Candy
    Orange Pecans, 132
    Sour Cream Fudge, 132
Cannelloni, 168
Caramel
    Brownies, 136
    Icing, 65
Carrot Cake, 74
Casserole(s)
    Garden Collage, 74
    Green Bean and Mushroom, 195
    Mushroom Eggplant, 78
    Shrimp and Artichoke Heart, 53
    Spinach, 193
    Squash, Broccoli or Spinach, 194
    Turnip and Onion, 123
Catfish, Fried, 75
Caviar Mousse, 99
Celery, Braised with Mushroom Purée, 191
Charlotte Russe, 121
Chateaubriand, 110
Cheese
    Ball with Pecans, 97
    Ball, Shrimp and, 135
    Biscuits, Twelve-Minute, 144
    Grits, 148
    Hot Balls, 142
    Roquefort Wafers, 141
    Soufflé, Cream, 87
    Soufflé, Original, 200
    Soufflé, Three, 201
    Straws, 126
Cherries Jubilee, 109
Chess Pie, Red Apple, 91
Chicken
    and Dumplings, 179
    Argolemono Soup, 154
    Breast Eden Isle, 81
    Breasts Minceur, 178
    Breasts with Ham, 176
    Breasts with Tarragon, 175
    Broiled Rock Cornish Game Hens, 181
    Cacciatore and Noodles, 180
    Cornish Hens Baked in Wine, 136
    Curried Salad, 158
    Divan, 175
    Filling for Crepes, 178
    Fried, Southern Style, 69
    Grilled with Dr. Shelton's Famous Basting Sauce, 72
    Kiev, Breast of, 180
    Liver Pâté, 120

Loaf, Hot, 114
Mulligatawny Soup, 100
Parmesan, 176
Pot Pie, 177
Salad Supreme, 50
Spaghetti, 179
Chili, Homemade, 59
Chocolate
    Angel Food Cake, 206
    Angel Food Cake Frosting, 206
    Angel Pie, 57
    Crème Fresche, 210
    Fudge Cup Cakes, 137
    Mousse, 116
    Roll, 94
    Sauce, 94
    Soufflé, 103
Christmas Quaii and Gravy, 131
Coconut
    Cake, 54
    Icing, 54
Codfish Balls with Grape Jelly, 41
Coffee Cake, 38
Cold
    Cucumber or Avocado Soup, 50
    Orange Soufflé, 51
    Rock Cornish Game Hens baked in wine, 136
Cole Slaw Mold, 93
Consommé, Jellied with Vegetables, 104
Cookie(s)
    English Toffee, 62
    Gun Dough, 207
    Macadamia Nut Balls, 63
    Pecan Meringues, 205
    Tuiles Aux Amandes, 63
Cool As a Cucumber Salad, 165
Corn
    Bisque, Crab and, 47
    Fritters, 57
    Pudding, 190
    Soup, Cream of Corn, 152
    Sticks, 48
Corn Bread
    Dressing, Eden Isle, 127
    Mexican, 145
    Salad, 162
    Skillet, 61
Cornish Hens Baked in Wine, 136
Crab
    and Corn Bisque, 47
    Artichoke Salad, 157
    Deviled Cakes, 185
    Deviled, 186

Noodles Italienne, 183
Soufflé, 56
Crab Meat
    Cucumber Ring with, 165
    Dip, Hot, 97
    Filling for Crepes, 185
    Mornay, Hot, 150
    Salad, 159
    Stuffed Eggplant with, 196
Cracker Balls, 60
Cream
    Cheese Soufflé, 87
    of Corn Soup, 152
Crème
    Brulée, 87
    Caramel, 113
    Fresche, 103
    Vichyssoise, 155
Creole Gumbo, 153
Crepes
    Blender, 150
    Orange, 206
Crepe Filling
    Chicken, 178
    Crab Meat, 185
Crisp Bacon, 36
Croutons, 113
Cucumber
    Mousse, 120
    or Avocado Soup, Cold, 50
    Salad, 135
    Salad, Cool as a, 165
    Sandwiches with Dill, 137
    Ring with Crab Meat, 165
Curried Chicken Salad, 158
Curry Mayonnaise, 158
Date and Nut Bread, 146
Desserts
    Apple Cake with Hot Buttered Rum Sauce, 59
    Apple Crisp, 71
    Bavarian Cream Pie, 210
    Boccone Dolce, 208
    Bread Pudding with Orange Sauce, 90
    Brownie Pie, 61
    Buttermilk Pound Cake, 65
    Caramel Brownies, 136
    Carrot Cake, 74
    Charlotte Russe, 121
    Cherries Jubilee, 109
    Chocolate Angel Food Cake, 206
    Chocolate Angel Pie, 57
    Chocolate Crème Fresche, 210
    Chocolate Fudge Cup Cakes, 137

Chocolate Mousse, 116
Chocolate Roll with Chocolate Sauce, 94
Chocolate Soufflé with Crème Fresche, 103
Coconut Cake with Coconut Icing, 54
Cold Orange Soufflé, 51
Cookie Gun Dough, 207
Crème Brulée, 87
Crème Caramel, 113
Crème Fresche, 103
Elna's Pumpkin Pie, 129
English Toffee Cookies, 62
Jam Cake with Caramel Icing, 65
La Fonda Pudding, 76
Lemon Angel Pie, 56
Lemon Christmas Cake, 133
Macadamia Nut Balls, 63
Mango Sherbet, 47
Orange Crepes, 206
Orange Pecan Pie, 78
Orange Soufflé, 210
Paradise Pie, 49
Pecan Meringues, 205
Pineapple Milk Sherbet, 68
Plum Pudding, 208
Red Apple Apple Pie, 84
Red Apple Chess Pie, 91
Rum Cake with Rum Sauce, 205
Russian Black Cherries, 207
St. Cecilia Sauce, 211
Shipp's Special, 207
Silk Pie, 209
Soufflé Grand Marnier, 211
Sour Cream Chocolate Cake, 64
Sour Cream Fudge, 132
Strawberry Shortcake, 124
Tuiles Aux Amandes, 63
Deviled
    Crab, 186
    Crab Cakes, 185
    Eggs with Asparagus, 137
    Oysters on the Half Shell, 186
    Rib Bones, 73
Dips
    Guacamole, 143
    Hot Crab Meat, 97
    Smoked Oyster, 98
Dr. Shelton's Famous Basting Sauce, 72
Dreamy Apricot Salad, 163
Duchess Potatoes, 111
Dutch Apple Bread, 145
Emerald Rice, 86
Eden Isle Corn Bread Dressing, 127

Egg(s)
    Deviled, with Asparagus, 137
    en Gelée, 164
    Fresh Herbed Omelet, 36
    Soft Scrambled, 39
    Sunday Brunch Mock Omelet, 38
Eggplant
    Casserole, Mushroom and, 78
    Scalloped, or Squash, 196
    Soufflé, 199
    Stuffed, with Crab Meat, 196
Elna's Pumpkin Pie, 129
English Toffee Cookies, 62
Emerald Rice, 86
Escargots, Mushrooms Stuffed with, 142
Filet Mignon with Bordelaise Sauce, 167
Filet of Sole Bon Femme, 189
Filling for Roquefort Wafers, 141
Fish and Seafood
    Artichoke Crab Salad, 157
    Avocado with Lobster Salad, 158
    Baked Red Snapper with Tomato Sauce, 189
    Broiled Trout with Maitre d'Hotel Butter, 188
    Caviar Mousse, 99
    Codfish Balls with Grape Jelly, 41
    Crab and Corn Bisque, 47
    Crab Meat Filling for Crepes, 185
    Crab Meat Salad, 159
    Crab Soufflé, 56
    Creole Gumbo, 153
    Cucumber Ring with Crab Meat, 165
    Deviled Crab Cakes, 185
    Deviled Crab, 186
    Deviled Oysters on the Half Shell, 186
    Filet of Sole Bon Femme, 189
    Fried Catfish, 75
    Fried Shrimp Amandine, 182
    Hot Crab Meat Dip, 97
    Hot Crab Meat Mornay, 150
    Jellied Clam and Beef Broth, 156
    Kulebiaka (Russian Salmon in Pastry), 118
    Lobster Chops, 187
    Lobster Salad with Thousand Island Dressing, 105
Mrs. Berry's Shrimp, 182
    Mushrooms Stuffed with Oysters, 141
    Noodles Italienne, 183
    Oysters Broiled in Bacon, 96
    Oysters Florentine, 55
    Pasta Shrimp Salad, 159
    Quick Seafood Curry with Indian Rice, 187
    Rich Oyster Stew, 152
    Salt Mackerel, 42
    Scalloped Oysters, 128

Scallops Rosemary, 184
Seafood Quiche, 188
Shrimp and Artichoke Heart Casserole, 53
Shrimp and Cheese Ball, 135
Shrimp and Scallop Brochettes, 184
Shrimp Aurora, 183
Shrimp Mousse, 45
Shrimp Rarebit, 183
Shrimp Salad, 160
Smoked Oyster Dip with Crudités, 98
Smoked Salmon Mousse, 142
Stuffed Eggplant with Crab Meat, 196
Trout Amandine, 85
Fluffy Arkansas Steamed Rice, 81
French
    Fried Onion Rings, 192
    Onion Soup, 154
    Sauce, 101
    Sour Cream Sauce, 143
    Style Boneless Leg of Lamb, 172
Fresh
    Fruit Salad with Poppy Seed Dressing, 57
    Herbed Omelet, 36
    Spinach Salad, 160
Fried
    Catfish, 75
    Chicken Southern Style, 69
    Quail and Gravy, 131
    Shrimp Amandine, 126
    Squash, 193
    Sweet Potatoes, 131
Frosting for Carrot Cake, 74
Frozen Fruit Salad, 161
Frozen Tomato Salad, 51
Fudge, Sour Cream, 132
Garden
    Collage, 74
    Salad with Oil and Vinegar Dressing, 48
Gazpacho, 155
Grand Marnier Soufflé, 211
Grapefruit and Avocado Salad, 129
Green Bean
    and Mushroom Casserole, 195
    Salad, 53
Green Beans, 93
Green Tomato Pickle, 69
Gremolata, 88
Grilled
    Chicken with Dr. Shelton's Famous Basting Sauce, 72
    Ham and Red Eye Gravy, 39
Grits
    Cooked in Chicken Broth, 39
    Cheese, 148

Guacamole Dip, 143
Gumbo, Creole, 152
Ham
    Baked, Eden Isle, 172
    Chicken Breasts with, 176
    Grilled and Red Eye Gravy, 39
    Loaf, 172
Hard Sauce, 208
Hearts of Palm Salad, 86
Hearts of Romaine Salad, 112
Hollandaise Sauce, 204
Homemade Chili, 58
Homemade Mayonnaise, 50
Horseradish Cream Sauce, 101
Hot
    Buttered Rum Sauce, 205
    Cheese Balls, 142
    Chicken Loaf, 114
    Crab Meat Dip, 97
    Crab Meat Mornay, 150
    Crackers, 101
    Mustard Sauce, 67
Hollandaise Sauce, 204
Hush Puppies, 76
Iced Danish Mary, 126
Indian Rice, 187
Irish
    Lamb Stew, 173
    Soda Bread, 54
Jam Cake, 65
Jean's Famous Rolls, 83
Jellied
    Clam and Beef Broth, 156
    Consommé with Vegetables, 104
Kale, Turnip Greens, Mustard and/or, 69
Kulebiaka (Russian Salmon in Pastry), 118
La Fonda Pudding, 76
Lamb
    French Style Boneless Leg of Lamb, 172
    Shanks, Braised, 88
    Spring, 123
    Stew, Irish, 173
Lemon
    Angel Pie, 56
    Christmas Cake, 133
    Muffins, 46
Lettuce, Wilted, 70
Lima Bean Mélange, 166
Liver, Chicken Pâté, 120
Lobster
    Chops, 187
    Salad, 105
    Salad, Avocado with, 158

Macadamia Nut Balls, 63
Maitre d'Hotel Butter, 188
Mango Sherbet, 47
Marinade for Shish Kebobs or Lamb Chops, 202
Marinated Tomatoes, 98
May Wine, 114
Mayonnaise, Homemade, 50
Meat Loaf, Mushroom Filled, 92
Mexican Corn Bread, 145
Molded Beet Salad, 119
   Mrs. Berry's Shrimp, 182
Mulligatawny Soup, 100
Mushroom(s)
   Casserole, Green Bean and, 195
   Duxelles, 106
   Eggplant Casserole, 78
   Purée with Braised Celery, 191
   Sauce, 115
   Stuffed, 111
   Stuffed with Escargots, 142
   Stuffed with Oysters, 141
   Stuffed with Spinach, 99
Mushroom-Filled Meat Loaf, 92
Mustard Greens, Turnip and/or Kale, 69
Noodles Italienne, 183
Omelet
   Fresh Herbed, 36
   Sunday Brunch Mock, 38
Onion(s)
   Rings, French Fried, 192
   Soup, French, 154
   Stuffed, 192
Orange
   Crepes, 206
   Cups, Sweet Potatoes in, 128
   Juice with Champagne, 130
   Nut Bread, 146
   Pecan Pie, 78
   Pecans, 132
   Sauce, 90
   Soufflé, 210
   Soufflé, Cold, 51
Original Cheese Soufflé, 200
Oyster(s)
   Broiled in Bacon, 96
   Deviled on the Half Shell, 186
   Dip, Smoked, 98
   Florentine, 55
   Mushrooms Stuffed with, 141
   Stew, Rich, 152
   Scalloped, 128
Pancakes, Buttermilk, 146
Paradise Pie, 49

Pasta
   Shrimp Salad, 159
   Vermicelli Angelo, 149
Pastry, 106, 118
Pâté Brisée, 177
Peach Salad Mold, Spiced, 115
Pea(s)
   Artichoke Bottoms and, 112
   Baby New Potatoes and, 115
   Black-Eyed, 69
   Soup, Purée of Split, 151
Peppers Sauté, 102
Perfection Mold, 124
Pecan(s)
   Cheese Ball with, 97
   Meringues, 205
   Orange, 132
   Pie, Orange, 78
   Salted with Rosemary, 96
   Waffles, 147
Pies
   Bavarian Cream, 210
   Brownie, 61
   Chocolate Angel, 57
   Elna's Pumpkin, 129
   Lemon Angel, 56
   Orange Pecan, 78
   Paradise, 49
   Pizza Supper, 148
   Red Apple Apple, 84
   Red Apple Chess, 91
   Silk, 209
Pineapple Milk Sherbet, 68
Pizza Supper Pie, 148
Plum Pudding, 208
Pone Bread, 71
Popovers, 37
Poppy Seed Dressing, 57
Pork, Roast Leg of Fresh, 171
Potato(es)
   Baby New, and Peas, 115
   Cakes, 42
   Dauphine, 191
   Duchess, 111
   Fried Sweet, 131
   in Orange Cups, Sweet, 128
   Soup, 151
   Winter's Night Casserole of Apple and Sweet, 193
Prime Rib of Beef, Roast, 101
Prune Sour Cream Coffee Cake, 43
Pudding
   Bread, 90
   Corn, 190

La Fonda, 76
Plum, 208
Pumpkin Pie, Elna's, 129
Quail and Gravy, Christmas, 131
Quiche, Seafood, 188
Quick
    Asparagus Dip, 143
    Seafood Curry, 187
Raisin Sauce, 203
Red Apple
    Apple Pie, 84
    Chess Pie, 91
Red Snapper, Baked, 189
Remoulade Sauce, 203
Reuben Sandwich, 67
Rice
    Emerald, 86
    Fluffy Arkansas Steamed, 81
    Indian, 187
    Salad, 73
Rich Oyster Stew, 152
Roast
    Leg of Fresh Pork, 171
    Prime Rib of Beef, 101
Roquefort
    Dressing, 166
    Filling for Wafers, 141
    Wafers, 141
Royal Anne Congealed Salad, 163
Rum
    Cake, 205
    Sauce, 205
Russian Black Cherries, 207
St. Cecilia Sauce, 211
Salad(s)
    Apricots or Green Gage Plum, 164
    Artichoke Crab, 157
    Asparagus Vinaigrette, 46
    Asparagus Mold, 89
    Avocado Mousse, 157
    Avocado with Lobster, 158
    Boston Lettuce with Walnut Dressing, 103
    Cabbage Slaw, 76
    Caesar, 82
    Chicken Supreme, 50
    Cole Slaw Mold, 93
    Cool as a Cucumber, 165
    Corn Bread, 162
    Crab Meat, 159
    Cucumber, 135
    Cucumber Mousse, 120
    Cucumber Ring with Crab Meat, 165
    Curried Chicken, 158

Dreamy Apricot, 163
Eggs en Gelée, 164
Fresh Fruit with Poppy Seed Dressing, 57
Fresh Spinach, 160
Frozen Fruit, 161
Frozen Tomato with Homemade Mayonnaise, 51
Garden with Oil and Vinegar Dressing, 48
Grapefruit and Avocado, 129
Green Bean, 53
Hearts of Palm, 86
Hearts of Romaine with Sour Cream Dressing, 112
Lima Bean Mélange, 166
Lobster with Thousand Island Dressing, 105
Molded Beet, 119
Pasta Shrimp, 159
Perfection Mold, 124
Rice, 73
Royal Anne Congealed, 163
Shrimp, 160
Shrimp Mousse, 45
Spiced Peach Mold, 115
Three-Tier, Molded, 161
Tomato Aspic Ring, 162
Wilted Lettuce, 70
Salad Dressings
    Curry Mayonnaise, 158
    for Cabbage Slaw, 76
    for Caesar Salad, 82
    for Corn Bread Salad, 162
    for Cucumber Salad, 135
    for Fresh Spinach Salad, 160
    for Green Bean Salad, 53
    for Marinated Tomatoes, 98
    for Wilted Lettuce, 70
    Mayonnaise, Homemade, 50
    Oil and Vinegar, 48
    Poppy Seed, 57
    Roquefort, 166
    Sour Cream, 112
    Thousand Island, 105
    Vinaigrette, 46
    Walnut, 103
    Yogurt or Sour Cream, 120
Salmon
    Kulebiaka, 118
    Mousse, Smoked, 142
Salt Mackerel, 42
Salted Pecans with Rosemary, 96
Sandwiches
    Cucumber, with Dill, 137
    Reuben, 67
    Tomato, 135
    Welsh Rarebit, 149

Sauces
    Basic Tomato, 204
    Basting, for Broiling Chickens, 202
    Béarnaise, 111
    Bordelaise, 167
    Chocolate, 94
    Chocolate Crème Fresche, 210
    Crème Fresche, 103
    Dr. Shelton's Famous Basting, 72
    for Spanish Omelet, 204
    French, 101
    French Sour Cream, 203
    Giblet Gravy, 127
    Hard, 208
    Hollandaise, 204
    Horseradish Cream, 101
    Hot Buttered Rum Sauce, 59
    Hot Mustard, 67
    Madeira, 108
    Marinade for Shish Kebobs or Lamb Chops, 202
    Mushroom, 115
    Orange, 90
    Quail Gravy, 131
    Raisin, 203
    Red Eye Gravy, 39
    Remoulade Sauce, 203
    St. Cecilia, 211
    Sour Cream, 92
    Tartar Sauce, 75
    Tomato, with Red Snapper, 189
Sauerkraut, 91
Scallops
    Brochettes, Shrimp and, 184
    Rosemary, 184
Scalloped
    Eggplant or Squash, 196
    Oysters, 128
Seafood Quiche, 188
Shipp's Special, 207
Shrimp
    and Artichoke Heart Casserole, 53
    and Cheese Ball, 135
    and Scallop Brochettes, 184
    Aurora, 183
    Fried, Amandine, 182
    Mousse, 45
    Mrs. Berry's, 182
    Pasta Salad, 159
    Rarebit, 183
    Salad, 160
Silk Pie, 209
Skillet Corn Bread, 61
Sliced Beef Tenderloin, 97

Smoked
    Oyster Dip, 98
    Salmon Mousse, 142
Soft Scrambled Eggs, 39
Sole, Filet of Bon Femme, 189
Soufflé
    Broccoli, 199
    Chocolate, 103
    Cold Orange, 51
    Crab, 56
    Cream Cheese, 87
    Eggplant, 199
    Grand Marnier, 211
    Orange, 210
    Original Cheese, 200
    Spinach, 82
    Squash, 201
    Three Cheese, 201
    Vegetable, 200
Soups
    Argolemono, 154
    Barley, 152
    Cold Cucumber or Avocado, 50
    Crab and Corn Bisque, 47
    Cream of Corn, 152
    Creole Gumbo, 153
    Crème Vichyssoise, 155
    French Onion, 154
    Gazpacho, 155
    Homemade Chili, 58
    Jellied Clam and Beef Broth, 156
    Jellied Consommé with Vegetables, 104
    Mulligatawny, 100
    Potato, 151
    Purée of Split Pea, 151
    Rich Oyster Stew, 152
    Tomato Basil, 110
    Tomato Madrilene, 155
    Vegetable, 60
Sour Cream
    Chocolate Cake, 64
    Chocolate Cake Icing, 64
    Dressing, 112
    Fudge, 132
    Sauce, 92
Sourdough Biscuits, 131
Spaghetti, Chicken, 179
Spiced Peach Salad Mold, 115
Spinach
    Casserole, 194
    Casserole, Squash, Broccoli or, 194
    Mushrooms Stuffed with, 99
    Salad, Fresh, 160

Soufflé, 82
Spoon Bread, 102
Spring Lamb, 123
Squash
    Baked Zucchini, 195
    Casserole, 194
    Fried, 193
    Scalloped Eggplant or, 196
    Soufflé, 201
    Stuffed, 194
Steamed Barley, 89
Strawberry
    Butter, 40
    Preserves, 37
    Shortcake, 124
Stuffed
    Eggplant with Crab Meat, 196
    Mushrooms, 111
    Squash, 194
    Tomato, 108
    Tomatoes, Baked, 190
Sunday Brunch Mock Omelet, 38
Succotash, 197
Sweet Potato(es)
    Casserole, Winter's Night of Apples and, 193
    Croquettes, 192
    Fried, 131
    in Orange Cups, 128
Tartar Sauce, 75
Thousand Island Dressing, 105
Three Cheese Soufflé, 201
Three-Tier Molded Salad, 161
Tomato(es)
    Aspic Ring, 162
    Baked Stuffed, 190
    Basic Sauce, 204
    Basil Soup, 110
    Croustades, 143
    Gazpacho, 155
    Madrilene, 155
    Marinated, 98
    Pickle, Green, 70
    Salad, Frozen, 51
    Sandwiches, 135
    Zucchini with, 55
Tournedos of Beef, 167
Trout
    Amandine, 85
    Broiled, 188
Tuiles Aux Amandes (Lacy Curved Almond Wafers), 63
Turkey and Giblet Gravy, 126

Turnip
    and Onion Casserole, 123
    Mustard, and/or Kale Greens, 69
Twelve-Minute Cheese Biscuits, 144
Veal Scallopini with Marsala, 174
Vegetable
    Soufflé, 200
    Soup, 60
Vermicelli Angelo, 149
Vinaigrette Dressing, 46
Waffles, Pecan, 147
Wassail, 133
Welsh Rarebit Sandwich, 149
William O. Douglas' Grilled Steak, 77
Wilted Lettuce, 70
Wine
    Cornish Hens Baked in, 136
    May, 114
Winter's Night Casserole of Sweet Potato and Apple, 193
Yogurt or Sour Cream Dressing, 120
Zucchini Squash, Baked, 195
Zucchini with Tomatoes, 55